THE COMPLETE CHRISTMAS COOKBOOK

MEREHURST

CONTENTS

STARTERS	4
MAIN COURSE DISHES	10
VEGETABLES WITH FLAIR	22
PUDDINGS & DESSERTS	26
TASTY TREATS	38
CHRISTMAS CAKES	42
THE MOST OF LEFTOVERS	56
FESTIVE CHEER	60
TABLE DECORATIONS	63
QUICK REFERENCE GUIDE	66
INDEX	71

ACKNOWLEDGEMENTS

The publishers would like to thank the following authors, photographers and publishers for the material used in this book: Mary Cadogan; Ming Veevers-Carter; Maxine Clark; J.B. Fairfax Press Pty Limited; David Gill; Carole Handslip; Ken Field; Janice Murfitt; James Murphy; Alan Newnham; Jenny Ridgwell; Lyn Rutherford; Jon Stewart; and Mandy Wagstaff.

Published in 1992 by Merehurst Limited, Ferry House, 51-57 Lacy Road, Putney, London SW15 1PR.

Reprinted 1993

Distributed by J.B. Fairfax Press Limited, 9 Trinity Centre, Park Farm, Wellingborough, Northants NN8 6ZB.

Copyright © Merehurst Limited 1992
Recipes on p.42 and p.48 copyright © Jane Asher
ISBN 1-85391-338-3 (cased)
1-874567-65-4 (paperback)

All rights reserved. No part of this publication may be reproduced, stored in a retrieval system, or transmitted in any form, or by any means, electronic, mechanical, photocopying or otherwise without the prior written permission of the copyright owner.

Edited by Katie Swallow
Designed by Grahame Dudley Associates
Cover photography by James Duncan
Cover food prepared by Joanna Farrow
Cover styling by Madeleine Brehaut

Typeset by Litho Link Limited
Colour separation by Fotographics Limited
U.K. – Hong Kong
Printed in Italy by G. Canale & C. S.p.A.

INTRODUCTION

The thought of Christmas approaching can put the most organized of cooks into a spin. There seem to be endless meals to prepare amidst all the other chaos of present wrapping and family organizing, while THE BIG MEAL itself looms ahead like some gigantic challenge.

With *The Complete Christmas Cookbook* to guide you through the long, hungry Christmas holiday, you can forget any worries about running out of good ideas to keep the family well fed and happy. One of the secrets of an enjoyable Christmas is to plan as much as possible in advance, and a few evenings sitting curled up with this book and a pen and paper will give you a head start.

From the large selection of tempting recipes there will be plenty to suit your family and guests, so start making lists early on. Don't forget to include some starters – you'll find something here to suit everyone, from the simple luxury of Smoked Salmon Parcels to the delicacy of Leek and Stilton Soufflés. And for those wary of cooking turkey, here is a foolproof method of producing Perfect Roast Turkey, along with ideas for all the trimmings you could possibly want.

We always like to have the Traditional Christmas Pudding at home, but it's lovely to offer something refreshing and tangy like the easy Lemon Mousse as an alternative. And after years of serving up depressing turkey rissoles, I really appreciate the delicious ideas for using up leftovers – who could resist the piquant Ham and Turkey Niçoise, or the delicious Turkey and Chutney Loaf?

If your children reach the same fever pitch of excitement as mine do as Christmas Day approaches, you could enlist their help in making some of the delicious little extras that add to the festive fun, like Chocolate Truffles and Christmas Tree Biscuits.

The Complete Christmas Cookbook also includes some simple ideas for creating beautiful, eye-catching decorations to add that elegant finishing touch to your Christmas table.

Finally, when you've prepared as much as you can, the stockings are up and the presents are wrapped, why not make yourself one of the wonderful cocktails featured in the book – perhaps a refreshing Champagne or Tropical Cup – then put your feet up and raise your glass in a toast – Happy Christmas!

Jane Asher

STARTERS

Awaken the palate for the Christmas meal to follow with one of these delectable starter ideas.

STRIPED SALMON TERRINE

375 g (12 oz) boned salmon, skinned
1 egg white
155 ml (5 fl oz) double cream
lemon juice to taste
salt and pepper to taste
375 g (12 oz) sole fillets, skinned
2 tbsp chopped dill
1 tbsp chopped tarragon or parsley
butter for greasing
salad leaves, herb sprigs and crème fraîche, to serve

Serves 4-6

1 Cut salmon into 2.5 cm (1 in) pieces, place in a food processor and blend until smooth. Add egg white and blend again until evenly mixed. Place in refrigerator and chill for at least 30 minutes.

2 Return salmon to food processor and add cream, lemon juice and salt and pepper. Blend until smooth. Chill for 30 minutes.

3 Cut sole fillets into long strips and roll in chopped herbs until well coated.

4 Preheat oven to 180°C (350°F/Gas 4). Grease a 625 ml (20 fl oz) loaf tin or terrine with butter. Spoon one third of the salmon mixture into the tin and spread evenly. Lay sole strips on top, leaving a border at each side. Carefully spoon remaining salmon mixture over sole and level the surface.

5 Cover with buttered foil and place in a roasting tin, containing enough hot water to come half-way up the sides of the terrine. Bake in oven for 35 minutes or until a fine skewer inserted into the centre comes out clean.

6 Lift terrine out of roasting tin and leave until cold. Remove foil, cover with oiled greaseproof paper and weight down. Chill for at least 4 hours before turning out. Cut into slices and serve with salad leaves, herb sprigs and crème fraîche.

LEEK & STILTON SOUFFLES

60 g (2 oz) butter
250 g (8 oz) leeks, finely chopped
2 tbsp plain flour
140 ml (4½ fl oz) milk
185 g (6 oz) blue Stilton cheese, grated
½ tsp powdered mustard
salt and pepper to taste
4 eggs, separated

Serves 4

1 Preheat oven to 190°C (375°F/Gas 5). Melt butter in a saucepan. Add leeks and sauté for 2-3 minutes until softened. Stir in flour and cook for 1 minute, stirring.

2 Remove pan from heat and gradually stir in milk. Return to heat and bring to the boil, stirring, until thickened.

3 Stir in grated cheese and mustard powder and season well with salt and pepper. Allow cheese sauce to cool slightly, then stir in egg yolks.

STARTERS

4 Whisk egg whites until stiff peaks form. Stir a little of the whisked egg whites into the cheese sauce to lighten the mixture, then fold in remainder; taking care not to overmix.

5 Spoon mixture into 4 oiled 315 ml (10 fl oz) individual soufflé dishes. Bake in centre of oven for 25 minutes until risen, golden brown and just firm. Serve immediately.

Clockwise from top right: *Ham & Asparagus Gratins; Striped Salmon Terrine; Leek & Stilton Soufflés; and Crispy Bacon & Avocado Salad.*

Ham & Asparagus Gratins

Illustrated on page 5

12 large asparagus spears
6 slices roast ham
30 g (1 oz) fresh white breadcrumbs
30 g (1 oz) flaked almonds

SAUCE

45 g (1½ oz) butter
45 g (1½ oz) plain flour
470 ml (15 fl oz) milk
90 g (3 oz) gruyère or mature Cheddar cheese, grated
2 tsp French mustard
salt and pepper to taste

Serves 4

1 For sauce, melt butter in a small saucepan. Add flour and cook for 1 minute, stirring. Remove pan from heat and gradually stir in milk. Return to heat and cook to give a smooth sauce, stirring. Stir in cheese and mustard and season with salt and pepper. Remove pan from heat.

2 Break off and discard woody ends of asparagus spears. Thinly peel stems using a potato peeler. Cook asparagus in a pan of boiling water for 4 minutes, then drain.

3 Preheat oven to 190°C (375°F/Gas 5). Cut ham slices in half and wrap each piece around an asparagus stem. Arrange ham and asparagus rolls in a lightly greased baking dish. Spoon over sauce and top with breadcrumbs and almonds. Bake in oven for about 20 minutes until sauce is hot and bubbling and topping is crisp and golden. Serve immediately.

Crispy Bacon & Avocado Salad

Illustrated on page 5

1 avocado
6 rashers of streaky bacon, chopped and rinds removed
250 g (8 oz) mixed salad leaves
60 g (2 oz) hazelnuts, chopped and toasted

DRESSING

3 tbsp hazelnut oil
1 tbsp cider vinegar
1 tsp French mustard
1 clove garlic, crushed
salt and pepper to taste

Serves 4

1 For dressing, put all the ingredients in a screw-topped jar and shake to combine.

2 Halve, stone and peel avocado. Slice into a bowl and pour over dressing, tossing until coated.

3 Dry-fry bacon until crisp, then add to bowl with salad leaves and hazelnuts. Stir until mixed. Serve immediately.

Crudites with Garlic Dip

2 red or yellow peppers
12 radishes
12 baby carrots
½ cucumber
125 g (4 oz) small mange tout
12 baby corn
2 sticks of celery
12 quail's eggs
herb sprigs to garnish

GARLIC DIP

8 tbsp good quality mayonnaise
2-3 cloves garlic, crushed
salt and pepper to taste

Serves 4-6

1 Prepare dip. Mix mayonnaise with garlic and salt and pepper to taste in a bowl.

2 Halve and seed the peppers and cut into long wedges. Trim the radishes, leaving on a little greenery at the ends. Peel and trim the carrots. Halve the cucumber lengthwise, scoop out the seeds and cut the flesh into sticks. Blanch mange tout and baby corn in boiling water for 1 minute: refresh in cold water and drain. Trim celery and cut into sticks.

3 Place the quail's eggs in a saucepan of cold water to cover and bring to the boil. Boil for 2 minutes, then plunge the eggs into cold water to cool. Partially peel the eggs.

4 Arrange the vegetables and eggs on a large platter or individual serving plates. Cover and chill until required. Garnish with herb sprigs and serve with garlic dip.

Smoked Salmon Parcels

2 hard-boiled eggs, finely chopped
125 g (4 oz) cream cheese
3 tbsp double cream
2 tsp snipped chives
salt and pepper to taste
4 slices smoked salmon
few whole chives
125 g (4 oz) mixed salad leaves
toast to serve

DRESSING

4 tbsp olive oil
2 tbsp lemon juice
½ tsp French mustard
pinch of sugar

Serves 4

STARTERS

1 Place eggs, cream cheese, cream and chives into a bowl and mix well. Season with salt and pepper.

2 Lay smoked salmon slices flat and divide cream cheese mixture between them. Roll or fold to enclose the filling. Tie each parcel with whole chives and refrigerate, covered with plastic wrap, until required.

3 For dressing, put all the ingredients in a screw-topped jar and shake to combine. Season with salt and pepper.

4 Just before serving, put salad leaves into a bowl, add dressing and toss gently to mix. Arrange salad leaves on individual plates with the salmon parcels. Serve with toast.

Above: *Smoked Salmon Parcels*

CHESTNUT & CRANBERRY SOUP

1 tbsp vegetable oil
1 onion, chopped
2 sticks celery, chopped
940 ml (1½ pints) vegetable stock
bouquet garni
salt and pepper to taste
500 g (1 lb) peeled cooked chestnuts, or can unsweetened chestnut purée
60 g (2 oz) cranberries
60 ml (2 fl oz) port
parsley sprigs and a few whole cranberries to garnish

Serves 6

1 Heat oil in a saucepan and sauté onion until softened. Add celery, stock, bouquet garni and seasoning. Bring to the boil, cover and simmer for 15 minutes.

2 Add chestnuts and cranberries to pan and simmer for 15 minutes. Discard bouquet garni. Allow soup to cool slightly, then blend in a food processor until smooth.

3 Return soup to pan, add port, adjust seasoning and serve garnished with parsley and cranberries.

COOK'S TIP

Fresh cranberries are becoming more widely available at Christmas time. Look out for them at larger supermarkets, or order them through your local greengrocer.

Mushroom Filo Tartlets

2-3 sheets frozen filo pastry, thawed
125 g (4 oz) butter, melted
1 clove garlic, crushed
2 shallots, finely chopped
375 g (12 oz) mixed mushrooms, wiped and chopped
4 tbsp white wine
salt and pepper to taste
herb sprigs to garnish

Serves 4

1 Preheat oven to 200°C (400°F/Gas 6). Cut filo pastry into twelve 10 cm (4 in) squares and brush liberally with melted butter.

2 Lay a filo square in each of four individual 7.5 cm (3 in) flan tins. Cover each of these with another filo square, moving tins a quarter-turn round. Repeat with remaining squares. Bake in oven for 8-10 minutes until golden. Keep warm.

3 Heat remaining butter in a frying pan, add garlic and shallots and sauté gently for 5 minutes until just turning golden. Add mushrooms and wine. Cook over a high heat for 2 minutes. Add seasoning.

4 Spoon filling into filo cases and garnish with herb sprigs. Serve immediately.

COOK'S TIP

To clarify butter, cut into cubes and melt slowly in a heavy saucepan over a low heat; do not allow to boil. Carefully spoon off the clear butter, leaving the milky sediment behind. Store clarified butter in refrigerator for up to 2 weeks.

Roquefort & Almond Soup

1 tbsp sunflower oil
1 clove garlic, crushed
1 tbsp plain flour
625 ml (1 pint) milk
60 g (2 oz) ground almonds
60 g (2 oz) Roquefort cheese
2 tbsp chopped chervil or parsley
salt and pepper to taste
chervil or parsley sprigs, and croûtons to serve

Serves 6

1 Heat oil in a saucepan, add garlic and sauté for 1 minute. Remove from heat and stir in flour, then 155 ml (5 fl oz) milk.

2 Add ground almonds to pan then add remaining milk. Return to heat and bring to the boil. Cook for 3 minutes until thickened.

3 Crumble in Roquefort, add herbs and cook gently until cheese has melted. Season. Serve with herbs and croûtons.

Cauliflower & Cress Soup

1 bunch watercress
2 tbsp vegetable oil
1 onion, chopped
1 small cauliflower, chopped
785 ml (1¼ pints) well-flavoured chicken stock
salt and pepper to taste
4 tbsp single cream
crusty bread to serve

Serves 6

1 Roughly chop watercress. Heat oil in saucepan, add onion and watercress, cover and cook gently for about 10 minutes until softened.

2 Add cauliflower, stock and seasoning. Bring to the boil, cover and simmer gently for 20 minutes until cooked.

3 Cool slightly, then pour into food processor and blend until smooth. Return to pan and heat through. Pour into individual serving bowls and swirl in cream. Serve with crusty bread.

Melon & Parma Ham

1 small Chanterais melon
1 small Galia or Ogen melon
12 very thin slices Parma ham

DRESSING

60 g (2 oz) dolcelatte cheese
juice of ½ lemon
1-2 tsp olive oil
1-2 tbsp cream or milk
pepper to taste
mint sprigs to garnish

Serves 4-6

1 Cut melons into thin wedges and arrange on individual serving plates with Parma ham. Cover and chill.

2 For dressing, mash dolcelatte and lemon juice to a paste, then stir in olive oil, cream or milk and pepper to taste.

3 Just before serving, spoon cheese dressing over melon and garnish with mint.

Chicken Liver Mousse

375 g (12 oz) chicken livers
salt and pepper to taste
1 tbsp Marsala or brandy
1 tbsp olive oil
250 g (8 oz) butter, softened
125 ml (4 fl oz) double cream
125 ml (4 fl oz) clarified butter, see Cook's Tip *left*
4 sage sprigs

STARTERS

Serves 4

1 Cut out and discard any bitter 'green' bits and any fatty 'strings' from livers. Rinse under cold water and pat dry with absorbent kitchen paper.

2 Sprinkle livers with salt and pepper. Place in a shallow dish with Marsala or brandy and olive oil. Cover and marinate for 1-2 hours, if time permits.

3 Place a non-stick frying pan over a low heat and add livers with marinade. Cook gently for 10-12 minutes or until livers are firm but still pink in the middle when pierced with a sharp knife; the livers should not brown. Cool slightly.

4 Place livers in a food processor and blend, gradually adding butter and working until smooth. Add cream and blend for 3 seconds. Adjust seasoning.

5 Spoon mousse into four individual ramekin dishes, smooth surface and cover each with a thin layer of clarified butter and a couple of sage leaves. Allow to set. Serve with salad leaves and melba toast.

Clockwise from top:
*Chicken Liver Mousse;
Mushroom Filo Tartlets;
and Melon & Parma Ham*

MAIN COURSE DISHES

Over the next few pages, you will find a host of delicious festive meat, poultry and vegetarian dishes.

PERFECT ROAST TURKEY

4.5 kg (9 lb) turkey (see pages 66-67 for useful information on preparing, cooking and carving the bird)
30 g (1 oz) butter, melted
a selection of vegetables, see page 22; Bacon-Wrapped Sausages, see page 12; Perfect Pan Gravy, see page 12; Spicy Cranberry Sauce, see page 13; and Bread Sauce, see page 13 to serve
sprigs of fresh rosemary and bay leaves to garnish

RICE & NUT STUFFING

315 g (10 oz) cooked brown rice
375 g (12 oz) minced pork or pork sausagemeat
½ bunch parsley, finely chopped
60 g (2 oz) flaked almonds, toasted
juice of 1 lemon
125 g (4 oz) sultanas
1 tsp dried mixed herbs
salt and pepper to taste

Serves 8

1 Place all the stuffing ingredients in a large bowl and mix until well combined.

2 Preheat oven to 190°C (375°F/Gas 5). Remove giblets and neck from turkey and put aside to make the gravy. Wipe turkey inside and out with damp kitchen paper, then dry.

3 Fill the neck cavity of the turkey with one-third of the stuffing. Do not pack tightly or the skin may split during cooking. Shape remaining stuffing into about 16 balls and place in an ovenproof dish. Chill until ready to cook.

4 Truss the turkey following instructions on page 66.

5 Place the turkey in a large roasting pan. Brush all over with melted butter and season with salt and pepper. Roast in oven for 2¼-2¾ hours until cooked, covering with foil any parts that brown too quickly. To test if the turkey is cooked, insert a metal skewer into the thickest part of both thighs. When cooked, the juices should run clear with no trace of pink.

6 When cooked, remove turkey from oven and allow to stand for 20 minutes.

7 Meanwhile cook stuffing balls in oven for 20-25 minutes until cooked and golden, covering with foil if necessary.

8 When ready to serve, remove trussing strings and skewer from turkey and place on a warmed serving plate. Arrange stuffing balls and other accompaniments around the turkey and garnish with herbs.

Perfect Roast Turkey served with a selection of festive vegetables; Bacon-Wrapped Sausages; Rice & Nut Stuffing Balls; Perfect Pan Gravy; Spicy Cranberry Sauce; and Bread Sauce.

Main Course Dishes

The Complete Christmas Cookbook

TURKEY ACCOMPANIMENTS

Traditional favourites to accompany the Christmas meal.

PERFECT PAN GRAVY

**giblets and neck from turkey
1 bay leaf
5-6 black peppercorns
few onion slices
few parsley stalks
salt and pepper to taste
1.2 litres (2 pints) water
4-5 tbsp roasting juices from cooking turkey
4 tbsp plain flour**

Makes about 1.1 litres (1¾ pints)

1 Place giblets and neck, bay leaf, peppercorns, onion, parsley, salt and water in a saucepan. Bring to the boil, then simmer for 1 hour. Strain, then reserve liquid.

2 Heat cooking juices from turkey in roasting pan over a gentle heat. Sprinkle flour over and stir with a wooden spoon until smooth.

3 Continue cooking and stirring until mixture turns a light golden colour. Gradually stir in reserved liquid. Increase heat to moderate and stir until gravy comes to the boil and is smooth and thickened.

4 Adjust seasoning. Pour into a warmed gravy boat.

BACON-WRAPPED SAUSAGES

**8 rashers of streaky bacon, rinds removed
16 small chipolata sausages**

Serves 8

Clockwise from top right: *Honey Apple Sauce; Spicy Cranberry Sauce; Cumberland Sauce;* and *Cherry Chutney.*

1 Preheat oven to 190°C (350°F/Gas 5). Hold each bacon rasher with one hand, and stretch it with the back of a knife. Cut the rasher in half.

2 Roll a half-rasher of bacon around each sausage. Place join-side down in a roasting pan and cook in oven for 20-25 minutes until cooked.

COOK'S TIPS

• *If preferred, the Bacon-Wrapped Sausages can be cooked under a preheated hot grill for about 5 minutes.*
• *As an alternative to the sausages, wrap bacon around no-soak dried prunes or cooked chestnuts.*

ALTERNATIVE STUFFINGS

OATY STUFFING BALLS

**500 g (1 lb) pork sausagemeat
1 onion, finely chopped
salt and pepper to taste
90 g (3 oz) medium ground oatmeal
2 tsp dried mixed herbs
salt and pepper to taste**

Serves 8

1 Preheat oven to 190°C (375°F/Gas 5). Put sausagemeat, onion and salt and pepper into a bowl and mix until well combined.

2 Shape stuffing into 16 small balls. Mix oatmeal with herbs and seasoning. Spread out on a plate and roll stuffing balls in oatmeal mixture.

3 Place stuffing balls in a greased ovenproof dish and bake for 20-25 minutes.

Apple & Hazelnut Stuffing

60 g (2 oz) butter
1 onion, chopped
1 kg (2 lb) cooking apples, peeled, cored and grated
finely grated rind and juice of 2 oranges
250 g (8 oz) fresh breadcrumbs
1 tbsp fresh chopped thyme
90 g (3 oz) hazelnuts, chopped
salt and pepper to taste
2 eggs, beaten

Sufficient to stuff neck cavity of a 4.5 kg (9 lb) turkey, and make 16 stuffing balls.

1 Melt butter in a saucepan, and add onion, apples and orange rind and juice. Cook until onion and apple are cooked. Remove pan from heat.

2 Mix breadcrumbs, thyme, hazelnuts and salt and pepper together in a bowl. Add apple mixture and beaten eggs and stir until well combined.

Cumberland Sauce

4 tbsp redcurrant jelly
1 tbsp marmalade
juice of 1 orange and ½ lemon
75 ml (2½ fl oz) port

Makes about 125 ml (4 fl oz)

1 Melt redcurrant jelly in a small saucepan over low heat. Stir in marmalade, orange and lemon juice, and port. Simmer for 1 minute.

2 Remove from heat and cool. Store in an airtight container in the refrigerator. Serve with pork or ham.

Bread Sauce

6 whole cloves
1 onion, peeled
1 bay leaf
625 ml (1 pint) milk
90-125 g (3-4 oz) fresh white breadcrumbs
60 g (2 oz) butter
salt and pepper to taste
large pinch ground nutmeg
2 tbsp single cream

Makes about 500 ml (16 fl oz)

1 Stick cloves into onion. Put onion, bay leaf and milk in a saucepan and bring to the boil. Remove from heat, then cover and set aside for 30 minutes.

2 Add breadcrumbs and butter to pan. Cook sauce over a very gentle heat for 15-20 minutes. Remove onion and bay leaf and add seasoning and nutmeg. Stir in cream just before serving.

Cherry Chutney

2 × 425 g (14 oz) cans pitted dark cherries
250 ml (8 fl oz) white vinegar
1 large onion, finely chopped
185 g (6 oz) granulated sugar
125 g (4 oz) sultanas
1 tbsp white mustard seeds
1 tbsp ground cinnamon
1 tbsp whole cloves
2 tsp salt

Makes about 625 ml (20 fl oz)

1 Drain cherries and pour the juice from 1 can into a medium-sized saucepan. Add the cherries and remaining ingredients to pan.

2 Bring to the boil, then cover and simmer gently for 1 hour, stirring occasionally. Remove lid and cook for a further 45 minutes, or until thick. Remove from heat and cool. Store in an airtight container in the refrigerator. Serve with ham, pork, duck or turkey.

Spicy Cranberry Sauce

350 g (10 oz) bottled cranberry sauce
1 tsp finely chopped fresh ginger
1 tsp ground cardamom
½ tsp cinnamon
2 tsp Worcestershire sauce

Makes about 250 ml (8 fl oz)

1 Place all ingredients in a small saucepan. Stir until mixture boils, then simmer for 1 minute. Allow to cool.

2 Store in an airtight container in the refrigerator. Serve with turkey or other poultry.

Honey Apple Sauce

3 Granny Smith apples, peeled, cored and diced
2 tbsp water
2 tbsp honey
15 g (½ oz) butter
1 tsp grated lemon rind
pinch of ground cloves

Makes about 500 ml (16 fl oz)

1 Place apples and water in a small saucepan with a tight-fitting lid. Bring to the boil, then cover the pan and simmer for about 5 minutes until apples are very soft and pulpy.

2 Remove from heat and beat in remaining ingredients. Store in an airtight container in the refrigerator. Serve with pork or duck.

The Complete Christmas Cookbook

Main Course Dishes

Honey-Glazed Ham

4.5 kg (9 lb) cooked leg of ham, see page 69
155 g (5 oz) clear honey
250 ml (8 fl oz) orange juice
1 tbsp French mustard
2 tsp soy sauce
1 tbsp soft brown sugar
whole cloves
watercress to garnish
pickles, mustard and Apricot & Orange Relish to serve

Serves 20-25

1 Preheat oven to 180°C (350°F/Gas 4). To remove the skin from the ham, start from the broad end of the ham, and gently ease skin away from the fat. Continue to peel off gently, and the skin should come off in one complete piece.

2 Hold ham firmly in one hand and, with a sharp knife, score the fat in a diamond pattern. Be careful to cut just through the fat, and not into the meat.

3 Place ham in a large roasting pan. Combine the remaining ingredients, except cloves, in a bowl, and brush about a quarter of the mixture over ham.

4 Stud each diamond in the fat with a whole clove. Place ham in oven and bake for 1 hour, brushing every 20 minutes with remaining glaze and cooking juices in roasting pan.

5 If serving the ham hot, allow it to rest for 5 minutes, then transfer to a warmed serving plate and garnish with watercress. If serving the ham cold, it may be glazed the day before and refrigerated, but allow to stand at room temperature for 20 minutes before carving. Cold meats are more succulent if not served straight from the fridge. Serve with pickles, mustard and Apricot & Orange Relish.

Apricot & Orange Relish

185 g (6 oz) dried no-soak apricots
315 ml (10 fl oz) unsweetened orange juice
2 tbsp white wine vinegar
1 tbsp clear honey
1 tsp cornflour
salt and pepper to taste
pinch of nutmeg or ginger

1 Place apricots in a saucepan with orange juice, vinegar and honey. Bring mixture to the boil, then simmer gently for 5 minutes until soft and pulpy.

2 Blend apricot mixture in a food processor until smooth, then transfer to a small pan and stir in cornflour.

3 Reheat mixture gently, stirring continuously until thickened. Season with salt and pepper and nutmeg or ginger. Serve relish hot or cold with slices of ham.

COOK'S TIPS

• *If you do not want to buy a ham this size, the same baking and glazing treatment can be given to a smaller ham.*
• *If preferred, you may like to remove some of the fat from the ham before glazing.*

The Complete Christmas Cookbook

French Roast Chicken with Cream Gravy

1.5 kg (3 lb) oven-ready chicken
fresh herbs and celery leaves to garnish

CHEESE MIXTURE

90 g (3 oz) cream cheese
2 tbsp chopped parsley
2 tsp chopped fresh tarragon or
½ tsp dried tarragon leaves
1 small onion, finely chopped
15 g (½ oz) butter, softened
salt and pepper to taste

STUFFING

30 g (1 oz) butter
1 small onion, finely chopped
2 sticks celery, finely chopped
2 tsp chopped fresh tarragon or
½ tsp dried tarragon leaves
2 tbsp chopped parsley
1 tsp grated lemon rind
125 g (4 oz) fresh white breadcrumbs

TO COOK CHICKEN

250 ml (8 fl oz) dry white wine
250 ml (8 fl oz) chicken stock
15 g (½ oz) butter

FOR GRAVY

375 ml (12 fl oz) cooking liquid from roasting
extra chicken stock, if necessary
1 tbsp cornflour, mixed with
125 ml (4 fl oz) cream
pinch of ground paprika

Serves 4

1 Preheat oven to 180°C (350°F/Gas 4). Remove excess fat from inside of chicken. Combine cheese with the parsley, tarragon, onion, butter and salt and pepper. With fingers, gently ease skin away from chicken breast. Push mixture over flesh.

Main Course Dishes

2 For stuffing, melt butter in a small saucepan and cook onion until softened. Combine with remaining stuffing ingredients. Spoon into neck cavity and close cavity with trussing pins.

3 Truss chicken, *see page 66*, and place, breast-side up, on a wire rack set in a flameproof roasting pan. Add wine, stock and butter to pan and roast chicken in oven for 1¼-1½ hours until crisp and golden and cooked; to test if the chicken is cooked, pierce thickest part of thigh with a skewer. When cooked, the juices will run clear. Baste frequently and turn the chicken 2 or 3 times during cooking. Roast breast-side up for the last 15 minutes.

4 To make gravy, transfer chicken to a warmed plate to rest for 5 minutes before carving. Place roasting pan on top of cooker and bring liquid in pan to the boil. If necessary, add extra stock to make 375 ml (12 fl oz). Stir about 60 ml (2 fl oz) of hot liquid into the cornflour mixture, then stir into pan. Continue stirring until smooth and thickened, and season.

Step 1

Step 2

5 Remove trussing pins and strings from chicken and carve chicken into 4 portions. Serve on heated plates with a little gravy spooned over. Serve remaining gravy separately sprinkled with paprika.

DUCK WITH ORANGE SAUCE

2.5 kg (5 lb) duck
1 orange and 1 lemon
salt and pepper to taste
1 small onion, chopped
few stalks of parsley
neck and giblets from duck
500 ml (16 fl oz) water

ORANGE SAUCE

3 tbsp sugar
60 ml (2 fl oz) vinegar
250 ml (8 fl oz) reserved duck stock
1 orange
1 tbsp arrowroot
125 ml (4 fl oz) port
2 tbsp Grand Marnier
15 g (½ oz) butter
orange slices and watercress or parsley to garnish

Serves 4

1 Preheat oven to 180°C (350°F/Gas 4). Remove excess fat from inside of duck, and wipe cavity dry with absorbent kitchen paper. Cut orange and lemon into quarters and place inside cavity. Season duck inside and out with salt and pepper, and truss, *see page 66*.

2 Place duck in a deep casserole dish with onion, parsley, roughly chopped neck and giblets and water. Cover the casserole and cook duck in oven for 1 hour, turning once or twice.

3 Remove duck, reserving liquid, and place breast-side up on a rack in a roasting pan. Increase oven temperature to 190°C (375°F/Gas 5). Return duck to oven and roast, uncovered, for 10 minutes, turn breast-side down and roast another 10 minutes, or until duck is golden brown.

4 Meanwhile, make sauce. Strain liquid from casserole dish and skim as much fat as possible from surface. Reserve 250 ml (8 fl oz). Place sugar and vinegar in a saucepan. Boil for a minute or two until thick and syrupy. Stir in reserved stock.

5 Carefully remove rind from orange with a vegetable peeler and cut into fine strips. Add to saucepan and bring to simmer. Squeeze juice from orange and mix with arrowroot. Add to sauce and stir until smooth and thickened.

6 Stir in port and Grand Marnier. Heat through but do not boil. Season to taste with salt and pepper and stir in butter.

7 Remove trussing strings from duck and place on a warmed serving dish. Spoon a little sauce over to glaze and serve the rest separately in a sauce boat. Garnish platter with orange slices and watercress or parsley.

COOK'S TIPS

- *To serve duck, cut in half lengthwise, then cut in half again crosswise – each dinner guest receiving a quarter of a bird.*
- *If cooking two smaller ducks, simply cut in half lengthwise and serve a half bird to each person.*

Roast Fillet of Beef with Port and Nut Stuffing

Fillet of beef with an orange and nut stuffing served with a rich port gravy.

1.5 kg (3 lb) fillet of beef, in one piece
watercress to garnish

STUFFING

30 g (1 oz) walnuts, coarsely chopped
30 g (1 oz) butter, melted
2 tbsp chopped parsley
2 tbsp clear honey
1 tbsp grated orange peel
60 ml (2 fl oz) port
1 egg, beaten
salt and pepper to taste
about 125 g (4 oz) fresh white breadcrumbs

TO COOK BEEF

1 large carrot, coarsely chopped
3 sticks celery, coarsely chopped
1 large onion, coarsely chopped
30g (1 oz) butter

GRAVY

250 ml (8 fl oz) beef stock
125 ml (4 fl oz) port

Serves 8-10

1 Preheat oven to 200°C (400°F/Gas 6). Trim the beef, removing all fat and sinews. Make a lengthwise incision to form a pocket for stuffing, cutting only three-quarters of the way through.

2 Combine all the stuffing ingredients, adding enough breadcrumbs to make a stuffing that is moist, but not wet.

3 Fill pocket with stuffing and tie beef at 5 cm (2 in) intervals with fine string to keep stuffing in place.

4 Scatter carrots, celery and onion in the base of a roasting pan and dot with butter. Place beef on top of vegetables. Roast in oven for 50-60 minutes for medium-rare beef, turning beef half-way through cooking time. Remove beef to a warmed serving plate, cover loosely with foil and allow to rest for about 15 minutes before carving.

5 Strain pan juices through a sieve into a saucepan, pressing down on vegetables to extract as much liquid as possible. Add beef stock and port to the saucepan and bring to the boil. Boil rapidly until liquid is reduced to thin gravy consistency. Season to taste with salt and pepper.

6 Remove strings from beef. Spoon a little gravy over the beef and garnish with watercress. Carve beef into neat, thick slices and serve remaining gravy separately in a warmed sauce boat.

> **COOK'S TIPS**
>
> *If preferred, vary the stuffing ingredients with whatever you have available. Replace the walnuts with Brazil nuts, cashew nuts or pine nuts; the parsley with tarragon or mixed herbs; the orange peel with lemon peel; and the white breadcrumbs with wholemeal breadcrumbs. You may need to add a little extra liquid if using wholemeal crumbs.*

Step 1

Step 2

Step 3

Step 4

Main Course Dishes

VEGETARIAN FILO SLICE

Whether you are a vegetarian or simply want something a little bit different to serve over the festive period, try this delicious layered vegetable filo slice.

---

375 g (12 oz) broccoli, cut into large pieces
500 g (1 lb) carrots, roughly sliced
125 g (4 oz) split red lentils
30 g (1 oz) butter
1 onion, roughly chopped
2 cloves garlic, crushed
125 g (4 oz) ground almonds
60 g (2 oz) mature Cheddar cheese, grated
4 eggs
1 red pepper, seeded and finely chopped
salt and pepper to taste
½ tsp curry powder
30 g (1 oz) fresh breadcrumbs
5 sheets filo pastry
oil for brushing
whole red chillies, parsley sprigs and Parmesan cheese to garnish

SAUCE

1 red pepper, seeded and chopped
2 cloves garlic, crushed
½ green or red chilli, seeded and sliced
15 g (½ oz) fresh breadcrumbs
5 tbsp olive oil

Serves 6-8

1 Preheat oven to 180°C (350°F/Gas 4). Grease and line a 1 kg (2 lb) loaf tin with greased greaseproof paper.

2 Cook the broccoli in a saucepan of boiling water until cooked, drain well. Cook carrots in a separate pan of boiling water for 10 minutes. Add lentils to carrots and cook for a further 10 minutes, drain well.

3 Melt butter in a pan and cook onion and garlic for 3 minutes. Place onions in a food processor and blend with broccoli and ground almonds to a smooth purée. Add cheese and 2 of the eggs. Beat until combined then stir in red pepper and season. Turn into prepared tin.

4 Blend carrots and lentils with remaining 2 eggs, curry powder, breadcrumbs and seasoning. Spoon into the tin. Using a teaspoon lightly swirl the two mixtures together. Cover with foil and bake in oven for 1 hour. Cool, then remove from tin.

5 Wrap loaf, like a parcel, in a sheet of pastry. Brush with oil and wrap with 3 more sheets of pastry, brushing each with oil.

6 Transfer the loaf to a baking sheet. Lay remaining sheet of pastry over loaf, easing pastry into soft folds. Brush lightly with oil and bake at 180°C (350°F/Gas 4) for 40 minutes, covering with foil once the pastry has turned golden.

7 Meanwhile make the sauce. Place red pepper, garlic, chilli and breadcrumbs in a blender and blend to a paste. Add the oil and blend until smooth.

8 Transfer loaf to a warmed serving plate. Serve sliced with sauce and garnished with chillies, parsley and Parmesan.

VEGETARIAN MENU

Chestnut & Cranberry Soup, see page 7
Vegetarian Filo Slice served with roast potatoes, *Beans with Tomato and Almond Brussels Sprouts*, see page 24
Easy Christmas Pudding, see page 28 served with *Orange and Brandy Butter*, see page 37

Main Course Dishes

21

VEGETABLES WITH FLAIR

Ring the changes this Christmas and try a selection of these colourful vegetable side dishes.

CITRUS BROCCOLI & CAULIFLOWER

250 g (8 oz) cauliflower, broken into florets
250 g (8 oz) broccoli, broken into florets

ORANGE SAUCE

125 ml (4 fl oz) fresh orange juice
2 tbsp tarragon vinegar
salt and pepper to taste
250 g (8 oz) unsalted butter
5-6 tbsp hot vegetable stock
orange rind shreds to garnish

Serves 4

1 Steam or cook cauliflower and broccoli florets in a saucepan of boiling salted water for 7-10 minutes until just cooked; drain and keep warm.

2 For sauce, place orange juice, vinegar and salt and pepper in a small saucepan. Bring to the boil and boil rapidly until reduced to 2 tbsp.

3 Remove pan from heat and whisk in butter, a piece at a time, until smooth and creamy. If the sauce becomes too thick, whisk very briefly over the heat.

4 Gradually whisk in enough stock to yield a pouring consistency. Pour sauce over vegetables and garnish with orange rind shreds.

ROSEMARY POTATOES

1 kg (2 lb) small old potatoes
4-5 sprigs rosemary
3 tbsp olive oil
coarse sea salt and pepper to taste
rosemary sprigs to garnish

Serves 6

1 Preheat oven to 200°C (400°F/Gas 6). Peel potatoes and make deep cuts on each, almost cutting right through. Strip rosemary leaves from stalks and chop them.

2 Place potatoes in a roasting pan and sprinkle with rosemary, oil and salt and pepper. Turn potatoes to coat thoroughly. Bake in oven for 1-1¼ hours until golden brown and cooked through. Serve garnished with rosemary.

Clockwise from top right: *Rosemary Potatoes; Almond Brussels Sprouts; Carrots & Celery;* and *Citrus Broccoli & Cauliflower.*

Vegetables with Flair

Beans with Tomato

500 g (1 lb) French beans
3 tbsp olive oil
2 ripe tomatoes, skinned and chopped
salt and pepper

Serves 4

1 Top and tail French beans, then rinse and drain. Cook beans in a saucepan of boiling salted water for 7-10 minutes. Drain well.

2 Heat oil in a pan, add tomatoes and cook gently for about 5 minutes. Add beans and stir well. Season. Cover and cook for 2-3 minutes.

> **COOK'S TIP**
>
> *To skin tomatoes, plunge into a bowl of boiling water and leave for 30 seconds, then peel.*

Roast Parsnips

750 g (1½ lb) small parsnips, peeled
salt
3 tbsp vegetable oil

Serves 4-6

1 Preheat oven to 200°C (400°F/Gas 6). Halve parsnips and parboil in a saucepan of boiling salted water for 5 minutes. Drain.

2 Heat oil in a roasting tin in oven. When hot, add parsnips and roast for 35-40 minutes until golden.

Almond Brussels Sprouts

Illustrated on page 23

500 g (1 lb) small Brussels sprouts
30 g (1 oz) butter
30 g (1 oz) flaked almonds
1 clove garlic, crushed
1 tsp finely grated lemon peel
1 tsp lemon juice
salt and pepper to taste

Serves 4

1 Trim stalks off sprouts and make a cross in each one. Cook in a saucepan of boiling salted water for 4-5 minutes until just cooked. Drain and keep warm.

2 Meanwhile, melt butter in a small frying pan, add flaked almonds and garlic and sauté until almonds are golden. Stir in lemon peel and juice and salt and pepper. Mix well.

3 Sprinkle almond mixture over sprouts and stir gently to mix. Serve immediately.

> **COOK'S TIP**
>
> *If preferred, replace flaked almonds with 90 g (3 oz) cooked whole chestnuts which have been sautéed in a little butter.*

Green Beans with Dijon Mustard

500 g (1 lb) French beans
salt to taste
30 g (1 oz) butter
1 tbsp chopped parsley
2 spring onions or 1 shallot, chopped
2-3 tsp Dijon mustard

Serves 4-6

1 Top and tail beans, then steam or cook in boiling water to cover for 5–10 minutes, until just tender. Drain if necessary, then sprinkle lightly with salt.

2 Melt butter in a saucepan, add parsley and spring onions and fry gently for 1 minute. Stir in mustard and 1 tbsp water. Add beans, turn to coat with sauce and heat through.

Celery with Bay & Bacon

1 head celery
salt and pepper to taste
30g (1oz) butter
1 small onion, chopped
2 rashers back bacon, chopped
2 bay leaves

Serves 4-6

1 Cut celery into 7.5 cm (3in) lengths, then into broad strips. Cook in boiling salted water to cover for 10 minutes. Drain, reserving 3 tbsp of the cooking liquid.

2 Heat butter in a saucepan, add onion and cook for about 5 minutes until softened. Add bacon and cook for a further 5 minutes, until bacon is slightly crispy. Add celery, bay leaves, salt and pepper, and reserved cooking liquid.

3 Bring to the boil, cover and cook gently for 20 minutes, until celery is tender. Serve hot.

CRISPY LEEKS

750 g (1½ lb) leeks
1 bouquet garni
2 cloves
15 g (½ oz) butter
125 ml (4 fl oz) vegetable stock
5 tbsp dry white wine
salt and pepper to taste
1 tbsp French mustard
1 tbsp dried brown breadcrumbs

Serves 4

1 Wash leeks and cut into 4 cm (1½ in) lengths. Place leeks in a saucepan with bouquet garni, cloves, butter, stock, wine and salt and pepper. Bring to the boil, cover and cook for 12-15 minutes until leeks are just cooked. Drain leeks, reserving cooking liquid.

2 Strain cooking liquid back into pan, then boil to reduce by half. Arrange leeks in a buttered shallow ovenproof dish. Add mustard to reduced cooking juices, stir well and pour over the leeks.

3 Preheat grill to moderately hot. Sprinkle breadcrumbs over leeks and grill until topping is crisp and golden.

PUFFED PARSNIP

500 g (1 lb) parsnips
salt and pepper to taste
60 g (2 oz) butter
3 tbsp cream
¼ tsp grated nutmeg
1 egg, beaten
2 tbsp breadcrumbs

Serves 4

1 Preheat oven to 180°C (350°F/Gas 4). Peel and halve parsnips, discard any woody cores and cut into chunks. Cook in a saucepan of boiling salted water for 15-20 minutes. Drain parsnips well.

2 Mash parsnips with half the butter, cream, nutmeg and egg. Season with salt and pepper. Turn mixture into a buttered ovenproof dish. Melt remaining butter and pour over top.

3 Sprinkle with breadcrumbs and bake in oven for 20-25 minutes until puffed up and golden brown.

CARROTS & CELERY

Illustrated on page 23

500 g (1 lb) carrots
4 celery sticks
1 small onion
½ red pepper, seeded
2 tsp olive oil
salt and pepper to taste
shredded spring onion to garnish

Serves 4

1 Peel carrots. Cut carrots and celery into even-sized sticks. Dice onion and pepper. Heat oil in a saucepan, add onion and sauté for 4-5 minutes until softened.

2 Add carrots and celery to pan and stir well. Cover pan and cook vegetables gently for about 10 minutes until vegetables are almost cooked, but still firm to the bite.

3 Stir in red pepper and season with salt and pepper. Sprinkle with spring onions and serve immediately.

> **COOK'S TIP**
>
> *This carrot dish is also delicious enhanced with 2 tsp chilli sauce. Add more chilli sauce if you prefer it hot.*

RAILROAD POTATOES

6-8 small baking potatoes
vegetable oil
salt

Serves 6-8

1 Preheat oven to 180°C (350°F/Gas 4). Peel potatoes and parboil them in a saucepan of boiling water for 5 minutes. Drain well and score surface all over with the prongs of a fork.

2 Pour enough vegetable oil into a small roasting pan to give a depth of about 1 cm (½ in). Add potatoes and sprinkle lightly with salt. Roast in oven for 40 minutes until crisp and cooked, turning and basting with oil occasionally during cooking.

Step 1

Step 2

PUDDINGS AND DESSERTS

All these festive specials can be prepared ahead of the meal so that you can relax with your guests and enjoy Christmas Day.

TRADITIONAL CHRISTMAS PUDDING

185 g (6 oz) plain flour
1 tbsp ground mixed spice
185 g (6 oz) shredded suet
125 g (4 oz) soft brown sugar
125 g (4 oz) fresh white breadcrumbs
grated rind and juice of 1 orange
1 cooking apple
90 g (3 oz) glacé cherries, roughly chopped
60 g (2 oz) flaked almonds
60 g (2 oz) hazelnuts
440 g (14 oz) currants
440 g (14 oz) raisins
375 g (12 oz) sultanas
60 g (2 oz) dried dates, chopped
4 eggs, size 3
250 ml (8 fl oz) brown ale
Orange & Brandy Butter to serve, see page 37

Makes 2 × 1 kg (2 lb) puddings
Each pudding serves 6-8

1 Grease and line bases of two 1 kg (2 lb) pudding basins with circles of greaseproof paper.

2 Sift flour and mixed spice together into a bowl. Add suet, sugar, breadcrumbs and orange rind and juice.

3 Peel, core and grate cooking apple, then add to bowl with cherries, nuts and fruits.

4 Lightly beat the eggs then add to the fruit mixture with the brown ale. Beat ingredients together until well combined.

5 Divide mixture between prepared basins and level surfaces. Cover with circles of greaseproof paper, securing under rims with string. Cover with foil and secure again with string.

6 Place puddings on upturned saucers in 2 large saucepans. Add 7.5 cm (3 in) boiling water to pans and cover with lids. Steam puddings for 6 hours, topping up with boiling water as necessary. Cool and cover puddings with fresh paper and foil.

7 Reheat as in step 6 for 3-4 hours. Turn out onto warmed serving plates and serve hot with Orange and Brandy Butter.

COOK'S TIPS

• *Keep a careful watch on the pudding as it steams to prevent the pan boiling dry, and top up with boiling water as necessary. Do not add cold water to the pan, as this will slow down the cooking time resulting in a soggy pudding.*
• *Before serving, push a foil-wrapped coin into the pudding; there is an old superstition that finding a piece of silver in the pudding indicates good fortune in the year ahead.*
• *To light the pudding, pour about 4 tbsp warm brandy over the pudding, then ignite with a match.*

Puddings & Desserts

EASY CHRISTMAS PUDDING

125 g (4 oz) butter or margarine
90 g (3 oz) soft brown sugar
2 eggs
185 g (6 oz) self-raising flour
1 tsp mixed spice
pinch of salt
155g (5 oz) mixed dried fruit
75 g (2½ oz) chopped dates
45g (1½ oz) glacé cherries, halved
4 tbsp sherry or orange juice
Fluffy Pineapple Sauce to serve, see right

Serves 6

1 Grease a 1 litre (32 fl oz) pudding basin. Cream butter or margarine and sugar until light and fluffy. Add eggs and beat well.

2 Sift flour with spice and salt. Fold into creamed mixture.

3 Add mixed fruit, dates, cherries and sherry or orange juice and mix well.

4 Spoon mixture into prepared pudding basin and cover with a tight-fitting lid or a double thickness of greaseproof paper or foil. If using paper or foil, tie securely in place with string.

5 Place basin in a saucepan on an upturned plate and add enough boiling water to come half-way up the sides of the pudding basin. Cover saucepan and steam pudding briskly for 2 hours. Add extra boiling water as necessary during cooking to keep the water level at the halfway mark.

6 Turn out pudding onto a warmed serving plate and pour a little Fluffy Pineapple Sauce over. Serve remaining sauce separately.

Pudding: Step 1

Step 2

Step 3

Step 4

FLUFFY PINEAPPLE SAUCE

2 eggs, separated
1½ tbsp lemon juice
4 tbsp cornflour
845 ml (27 fl oz) unsweetened pineapple juice
4 tbsp brown sugar

Serves 6

1 Beat together the egg yolks, lemon juice and cornflour until smooth.

2 Heat pineapple juice and brown sugar to simmering point. Gradually stir in cornflour mixture and continue stirring over low heat until mixture is smooth and thickened. Simmer for 2 minutes. Remove from heat and cool. Pour into a bowl.

3 Beat egg whites until stiff and fold into pineapple sauce. Serve immediately, or cover and chill until required, then reheat gently.

COOK'S TIP

If you have any left over, this light, tangy sauce is also delicious served chilled with ice-cream.

Puddings & Desserts

The Complete Christmas Cookbook

CHESTNUT BAVAROIS

7 g (¼ oz) powdered gelatine
250 ml (8 fl oz) milk
250 g (8 oz) can unsweetened chestnut purée
3 egg yolks
90 g (3 oz) caster sugar
470 ml (15 fl oz) whipping cream
whipped cream and 4 marrons glacés to decorate

Serves 6

1 Chill a 940 ml (1½ pint) charlotte tin. Soak gelatine in 1 tbsp water until spongy. Place milk and half the chestnut purée in a saucepan and bring to the boil.

2 Whisk together egg yolks and 60 g (2 oz) of the sugar until thick and light. Stir in a little of the hot milk, then add remaining milk in the pan and cook until custard thickens enough to coat back of the spoon, stirring constantly. Do not allow to boil.

3 Add soaked gelatine to hot custard. Chill until on the point of setting.

4 Whip cream until soft peaks form and set aside. Place remaining chestnut purée in a small bowl and break up with a fork. Add remaining sugar and beat until smooth. Fold in 2 tbsp of the chilled custard and 1 tbsp of the cream. Set aside.

5 Fold remaining cream into chilled custard and pour half of this into charlotte tin. Chill until set. Spoon chestnut purée onto the set bavarois and spread evenly with back of spoon. Top with remaining bavarois mixture and chill until completely set.

6 To unmould bavarois, run point of knife around top edge. Dip mould into hot water for a few seconds, then invert onto a chilled plate. Decorate with cream and marrons glacés and serve immediately.

LEMON MOUSSE

375 ml (12 fl oz) condensed milk
315 ml (10 fl oz) whipping cream
grated rind and juice of 4 large lemons
lemon slices and mint sprigs to decorate

Serves 6-8

1 Put condensed milk and cream into a large bowl and whisk with an electric beater until thick enough to leave a ribbon trail.

2 Continue to whisk mixture and slowly add lemon rind and juice; the mixture will suddenly thicken.

3 Spoon mixture into individual serving dishes and chill overnight. Decorate with lemon slices and mint sprigs.

> **COOK'S TIP**
>
> *This refreshing lemon mousse is equally as delicious made with other citrus fruit. Simply replace grated rind and juice of lemons with that of 4 small oranges, or 6 limes. Vary the decoration accordingly.*

Clockwise from top right: *Lemon Mousse; Chestnut Bavarois; and Iced Cointreau Soufflé.*

ICED COINTREAU SOUFFLE

Illustrated on page 30

3 eggs
2 egg yolks
155 g (5 oz) caster sugar
grated rind and juice of
1 orange
315 ml (10 fl oz) whipping cream
75 ml (2½ fl oz) Cointreau
orange segments and orange
rind shreds to decorate

Serves 10

1 Cut a piece of non-stick baking paper at least 25 cm (10 in) deep and long enough to wrap around a 625 ml (1 pint) soufflé dish. Fold paper in half lengthways to give a 12 cm (5 in) band. Wrap this around dish and secure with a piece of string. The collar should stand about 5 cm (2 in) above top of dish.

2 Place whole eggs, egg yolks, sugar, orange rind and juice in a large heatproof bowl. Stand bowl over a pan of hot water and whisk continuously using an electric whisk if possible, until mixture forms a thick ribbon when whisk is lifted.

3 Remove bowl from pan and whisk until mixture is cool.

4 Whip cream until it is the same consistency as the whisked mixture, then fold a spoonful of cream into the mixture. Fold in remaining cream and Cointreau. Pour mixture into prepared dish and freeze overnight.

5 To serve, carefully remove paper collar, smooth edge and decorate with orange segments and orange rind shreds.

FESTIVE POACHED PEARS

6 pears
3 figs
2 seedless oranges
1 pomegranate, optional
whipped cream to serve

SYRUP

2 bottles red wine
1 cinnamon stick
4 cloves
4 green cardamom pods
1 bay leaf
1 star anise
2 coriander seeds
2 white peppercorns
1 cm (½ in) fresh root ginger,
thinly sliced
90 g (3 oz) soft brown sugar

Serves 6

1 For syrup, pour wine into a large saucepan, bring to the boil and simmer, uncovered, until reduced by one third.

2 Tie spices in a square of muslin and add to the wine with ginger and sugar. Continue to simmer until liquid is reduced to half its original volume.

3 Peel and halve pears, then scoop out cores, using a melon baller. Add pears to wine, cover with a disc of greaseproof paper and simmer for 15-20 minutes until pears are cooked.

4 Quarter figs, then add to hot syrup and leave to cool, so they absorb the flavours.

5 Peel and segment oranges. Halve pomegranate if using and scoop out flesh.

6 Lift pears and figs out of the syrup and place in a serving bowl with oranges and pomegranate. Strain syrup; taste and add a little more sugar if necessary. Pour syrup over fruit. Serve with whipped cream.

CRUNCHY CHOCOLATE SLICE

60 g (2 oz) butter
500 g (1 lb) dark chocolate
75 ml (2½ fl oz) strong
black coffee
1 tbsp golden syrup
1 tbsp rum
125 g (4 oz) mixed nuts
250 g (8 oz) shortbread
125 g (4 oz) dates, stoned and
chopped
125 g (4 oz) glacé cherries,
halved
1 banana, roughly chopped

TO DECORATE

6 glacé cherries, halved and
strips of angelica

Serves 8

1 Grease a 750 g (1½ lb) loaf tin. Place butter, chocolate, coffee, syrup and rum in a heat-proof bowl over a pan of simmering water and heat gently until chocolate is melted. Remove from heat and stir until smooth.

2 Roughly break up nuts and half the shortbread. Crush remaining shortbread.

3 Add dates, cherries, banana, nuts and all of the shortbread to the chocolate mixture and stir well. Spoon into prepared tin and level top. Cover and chill overnight.

4 To serve, run point of a small knife around sides of the tin and invert onto a serving plate. Decorate top with cherries and angelica. Cut into thin slices to serve.

MERINGUE NESTS

3 egg whites
large pinch cream of tartar
220 g (7 oz) caster sugar
whipped cream and fresh fruit to serve

Makes 12 meringue nests

1 Preheat oven to 120°C (250°F/Gas½). Line 2 baking trays with non-stick baking paper. Using an upturned glass or cup as a guide, draw 12 circles about 6 cm (2½ in) in diameter on the paper. Beat egg whites until frothy, then add cream of tartar and beat until whites stand in stiff peaks.

2 Gradually beat in 2 tablespoons of the sugar. Continue beating for about 2 minutes until meringue is stiff and glossy.

3 Sprinkle remaining sugar over the top and fold through quickly and lightly with a metal tablespoon.

4 Spoon meringue into a piping bag fitted with a large plain or star tube. Pipe meringue to fill in circles on baking paper, then pipe circles around edges to form nests.

5 Bake meringues in oven for 1 hour. Turn off oven. Turn shells upside down on baking trays and return to turned-off oven. Leave in oven until cool.

6 Fill with whipped cream and fruit of your choice just before serving. Do not fill meringues in advance or they will soften.

COOK'S TIPS

- *Once you try homemade meringues, you'll want to serve them often! Happily, despite their fragile appearance and melting texture, they keep very well for up to 2 weeks in an airtight container.*
- *You can also vary the size and shape of the meringue nests. Instead of round nests, make them square or holly-leaf shaped – just cut stencils from stiff cardboard and draw around them on the baking paper.*

ICED CHRISTMAS PUDDING

60 g (2 oz) each of sultanas, currants and raisins
125 g (4 oz) chopped glacé cherries
60g (2 oz) chopped mixed dried peel
30 g (1 oz) chopped glacé pineapple or stem ginger
60 ml (2 fl oz) brandy
1 litre (32 fl oz) vanilla ice-cream
155 ml (5 fl oz) double cream
125 g (4 oz) flaked almonds, toasted
60 g (2 oz) chocolate chips
sieved cocoa powder, chocolate holly leaves and marzipan berries to decorate, see Cook's Tips

Serves 10-12

1 Mix dried fruits with brandy. Cover with plastic wrap and leave for several hours.

2 Soften ice-cream and place in a bowl with cream. Stir in fruits, almonds and chocolate chips.

3 Spoon into a 1.75 litre (3 pint) pudding basin and cover with freezer wrap. Freeze overnight.

4 Remove freezer wrap and immerse basin in hot – not boiling water for 20 seconds. Unmould pudding onto a chilled serving plate and decorate.

Pudding: Step 1

Step 2

Step 3

COOK'S TIPS

- *To make chocolate leaves, wash and dry several holly leaves. Brush backs of leaves with melted chocolate and refrigerate, chocolate side up, on a baking sheet lined with non-stick baking paper. When chocolate is set, carefully peel leaves off chocolate. The holly berries are made from balls of red marzipan.*
- *If you would like a dark pudding, simply use chocolate ice-cream in place of vanilla. Strawberry ice-cream would create a pretty pink pudding.*

APRICOT SHERRY TRIFLE

440 g (14 oz) pkt sponge rolls
125 ml (4 fl oz) sweet sherry, Marsala or port
2 × 411 g (14½ oz) cans apricot halves, drained
500 ml (16 fl oz) prepared custard
142 g (4 oz) packet raspberry or strawberry jelly made up according to instructions and set in a shallow tin
300 ml (½ pint) double cream
fresh fruit and chopped nuts to decorate

Serves 6-8

1 Cut sponge rolls into 1 cm (½ in) slices and use half the slices to line base and sides of a glass bowl. Sprinkle slices with half the sherry, Marsala or port.

2 Arrange half the apricots on top of cake and cover with half the custard.

3 Chop jelly into cubes and sprinkle half over the custard. Place another layer of cake slices on top, moisten with remaining sherry, Marsala or port. Add another layer of apricots, custard and jelly.

4 Beat cream until thick and fill a piping bag. Pipe cream in a lattice pattern over top of trifle and decorate with fruit and nuts. Chill until ready to serve.

COOK'S TIP

Trifle is always a family favourite, but you might like to make younger children a small 'special' version without alcohol. In this case, simply sprinkle the cake layers with juice from canned apricots, or orange or pineapple juice.

The Complete Christmas Cookbook

Puddings & Desserts

Egg Custard

750 ml (24 fl oz) milk
3 tbsp caster sugar
1 tbsp cornflour
2 eggs
pinch of salt
1½ tsp vanilla essence

Serves 6-8

1 Bring milk to the boil over gentle heat. Meanwhile, beat together sugar, cornflour, eggs and salt in a large bowl.

2 Whisk about 60 ml (2 fl oz) of boiling milk into egg mixture. Return to saucepan.

3 Continue cooking over gentle heat, beating all the time with a wooden spoon until custard is smooth and thick. Simmer for 1 minute, still beating. Remove from heat and stir in vanilla essence. If not serving custard immediately, cover top with a circle of damp greaseproof paper.

Step 1

Step 2

Orange & Brandy Butter

125 g (4 oz) unsalted butter, at room temperature
155 g (5 oz) icing sugar, sifted
2 tsp grated orange rind, optional
1 tbsp brandy or rum

Serves 6-8

1 Cream butter until very light and fluffy.

2 Gradually beat in icing sugar and continue beating until mixture is white in colour. Beat in orange rind if using, then brandy or rum. Cover with plastic wrap and store in the refrigerator until required.

Step 1

Step 2

Clear Brandy Sauce

90 g (3 oz) soft brown sugar
2 tbsp cornflour
pinch of salt
500 ml (16 fl oz) water
2.5 cm (1 in) cinnamon stick
6 whole cloves
30 g (1 oz) butter
60 ml (2 fl oz) brandy

Serves 6-8

1 In a medium saucepan, away from heat, combine brown sugar, cornflour and salt. Gradually stir in water.

2 Place over moderate heat and add cinnamon stick and cloves. Bring to the boil, stirring. Reduce heat and simmer for 3 minutes. Remove cinnamon and cloves. Stir in butter and enough brandy to give desired flavour. Serve hot.

Step 1

Step 2

TASTY TREATS

Christmas would not be complete without all the little extras that add to the fun. Easy to make and always appreciated.

MINCE PIES

MINCEMEAT

125 g (4 oz) each currants, sultanas and raisins
125 g (4 oz) chopped mixed dried peel
125 g (4 oz) shredded suet
90 g (3oz) almonds, chopped
1 large Granny Smith apple, peeled, cored and grated
juice and grated rind of 2 lemons
juice and grated rind of 1 large orange
227 g (8 oz) can crushed pineapple, drained, optional
60 g (2 oz) soft brown sugar
1 tsp mixed spice
60 ml (2 fl oz) brandy

PASTRY

125 g (4 oz) butter
125 g (4 oz) caster sugar
1 egg
125 g (4 oz) self-raising flour
125 g (4 oz) plain flour
1 egg white, lightly beaten

Makes 12 pies

1 For mincemeat, combine all ingredients. Spoon into jars with tight-fitting lids and store in the refrigerator until required. The flavour of fruit mince develops and grows richer with time, so try to store for at least a week before baking pies.

2 For pastry, cream butter and sugar. Add egg and beat in. Sift flours and fold in. Knead lightly, wrap in plastic wrap and chill for 1 hour. Preheat oven to 180°C (350°F/Gas 4). Roll dough out on a floured surface and cut out twelve 7.5 cm (3 in) rounds with a fluted pastry cutter.

3 Fit rounds into well-greased or non-stick tartlet cases or patty tins. Spoon filling into cases. From remaining pastry, cut lids, see Cook's Tips. Brush lids with egg white and bake pies in oven for 25 minutes, or until pastry is golden. Cool in the tins for a minute before removing to wire racks.

Clockwise from top right: *Mince Pies; Christmas Tree Biscuits; and Chocolate Truffles.*

COOK'S TIPS

- *For citrus pastry add grated rind of 1 orange or lemon in Step 2. Alternatively, replace 60 g (2 oz) of plain flour with ground almonds.*
- *Add interest to the pies by decorating in various ways. Use biscuit cutters to cut out star, holly leaf or angel shapes; or lattice strips of pastry over the mincemeat. For plain lids, make a small hole in the top of the pie to allow steam to escape during cooking.*
- *Mince pies are best served warm dusted with icing sugar.*

CHOCOLATE TRUFFLES

250 g (8 oz) dark chocolate, broken into pieces
1½ tbsp instant coffee powder
3 tbsp hot water
125 g (4 oz) unsalted butter, cut into small pieces
3 tbsp coffee or chocolate-flavoured liqueur
about 60 g (2 oz) cocoa powder
25 small paper cases

Makes about 25 truffles

TASTY TREATS

1 Place chocolate, coffee powder and hot water in a heatproof bowl over a pan of simmering water. Stir until chocolate melts then remove bowl from heat.

2 Have butter at room temperature. Using a wire whisk, beat butter into chocolate mixture a piece at a time. When all butter is incorporated, beat in liqueur. Cover bowl and chill mixture until firm.

3 Sift cocoa onto a sheet of greaseproof paper. Using a teaspoon, take out walnut-sized pieces of mixture and shape them into balls.

4 Roll balls in cocoa, then transfer to paper cases. Refrigerate until ready to serve.

COOK'S TIPS

- Tiny bottles of liqueur are a good buy for recipes requiring only 2 or 3 tablespoons. The truffles can also be flavoured with brandy, whisky or sherry if you already have a bottle.
- If preferred, roll truffles in finely grated white or dark chocolate, toasted coconut or finely chopped mixed nuts.

CHRISTMAS TREE BISCUITS

Illustrated on page 39

375 g (12 oz) plain flour
2 tsp baking powder
2 tsp cinnamon
1 tsp mixed spice
1 tsp ground ginger
¼ tsp salt
250 g (8 oz) butter, softened
185 g (6 oz) soft brown sugar
3 tbsp brandy, rum or orange juice
1 egg white, lightly beaten
sultanas, raisins, almonds and glacé cherries to decorate

Makes about 45 biscuits

1 Preheat oven to 180°C (350°F/Gas 4). Sift together flour, baking powder, cinnamon, spice, ginger and salt and set aside. Cream butter with an electric mixer or wooden spoon and gradually beat in sugar. Add brandy, rum or orange juice, then dry ingredients. Stir until well combined and a soft dough forms. Wrap in plastic wrap and chill for 30 minutes.

2 Turn out dough onto a lightly floured surface and roll out with a floured rolling pin to make a rectangle about 5 mm (¼ in) thick. Cut dough into shapes with decorative biscuit cutters.

3 Arrange biscuits on greased baking trays and brush with egg white. Use a metal skewer to mark patterns on each biscuit and decorate with sultanas, raisins, almonds and cherries. Make a hole in the top of each for threading ribbon. Bake in oven for 15 minutes or until firm to touch. Transfer biscuits onto a wire rack to cool.

4 Store biscuits in an airtight container. To decorate, thread ribbon through holes in biscuits and tie to branches.

FRUIT AND NUT CARAMELS

185 g (6 oz) glacé cherries, chopped
90 g (3 oz) dried apricots, chopped
155g (5 oz) whole mixed nuts
220 g (7 oz) caster sugar
90 g (3 oz) butter or margarine
2 tbsp golden syrup
4 tbsp liquid glucose
125 ml (4 fl oz) condensed milk

Makes about 70 pieces

1 Grease a 28 × 18 cm (11 × 7 in) cake tin. Spread cherries, apricots and mixed nuts evenly over the base of the tin.

2 Place the remaining ingredients in a heavy-based saucepan and heat gently, stirring constantly until sugar dissolves. Raise heat to moderate and continue cooking and stirring the mixture for about 10 minutes until it turns a dark golden colour and begins to come away from the sides of the saucepan.

3 Pour caramel mixture over fruit and nuts and leave for about 1 hour until set. When set, chop into small pieces using a cleaver or heavy knife and store in an airtight container.

4 Arrange in pretty paper cases on a festive doily.

Step 1

Step 2

Step 3

SHORTBREAD JEWELS

250 g (8 oz) butter, cut into small pieces
155 g (5 oz) caster sugar
60 g (2 oz) ground rice
375 g (12 oz) plain flour, sifted
60 g (2 oz) each red and green glacé cherries
125 g (4 oz) blanched almonds

Makes 24 biscuits

1 Preheat oven to 160°C (325°F/Gas 3). Lightly grease a 30 × 25 cm (12 × 10 in) shallow Swiss roll tin. Rub butter and sugar together in a bowl.

2 Gradually work in the ground rice, then the plain flour, until mixture forms a ball.

3 Press dough evenly into the prepared tin and mark lightly into 5 cm (2 in) squares. Decorate each square with cherries and almonds. Bake in oven for 40 minutes, or until golden.

4 Cool shortbread before cutting into squares.

CHEESE-PECAN CRISPS

60 g (2 oz) plain flour
60 g (2 oz) self-raising flour
pinch of salt
generous pinch of ground chilli
60 g (2 oz) butter
185 g (6 oz) Cheddar cheese, finely grated
60 g (2 oz) walnuts, finely chopped
2 tbsp beer or water

Serves 6-8

1 Preheat oven to 180°C (350°F/Gas 4). Sift flours, salt and chilli into a bowl. Rub in butter until mixture resembles breadcrumbs. Stir in cheese and walnuts.

2 Add beer or water and mix to a dough. Chill for 30 minutes, then roll out thinly on a lightly floured surface. Cut into small rounds. Bake on lightly greased baking trays for about 15 minutes until crisp. Cool, then store in an airtight container.

Step 1

Step 2

MARINATED MUSHROOMS

500 g (1 lb) button mushrooms
375 ml (12 fl oz) water
2 tbsp lemon juice
60 ml (2 fl oz) olive oil
60 ml (2 fl oz) cider vinegar
1 tbsp dried mixed peppercorns
1 tsp finely chopped garlic
1 tsp caster sugar
1 bay leaf
salt to taste
a few sprigs fresh dill, tarragon or oregano

Serves 6-8

1 Trim mushroom stalks and wipe caps with damp kitchen paper. Put in a saucepan with water and lemon juice and bring to boil. Cook for 1 minute; drain.

2 Place mushrooms in a jar with a tight-fitting lid. Combine the remaining ingredients and pour over mushrooms. The liquid should cover them completely. Store in the refrigerator for a week before serving.

Step 1

Step 2

SAUSAGE ROLLS

625 g (1¼ lb) puff pastry, thawed if frozen
500 g (1 lb) lean pork sausage meat
1 tsp dried mixed herbs
salt and pepper to taste
1 egg, beaten

Makes 18

1 Preheat oven to 220°C (425°F/Gas 7). Roll out pastry on a lightly floured surface to a rectangle measuring 46 × 15 cm (18 × 6 in). Cut pastry in half to give 2 strips 7.5 cm (3 in) wide.

2 Place sausage meat in a bowl and mix in herbs and salt and pepper. Divide sausage meat in half and shape each half into a long roll.

3 Lay a roll of sausage meat in the centre of each pastry strip and brush the edges of the pastry with beaten egg. Fold pastry over and seal long edges.

4 Brush sausage rolls with egg, then cut into 5 cm (2 in) pieces. Score top of sausage rolls, then transfer to 2 baking sheets and bake in oven for 25-30 minutes until pastry is crisp and golden.

COOK'S TIP

Vary the sausage meat filling by adding other flavouring ingredients. Replace the mixed herbs with other herbs of your choice; add 30 g (1 oz) chopped mixed nuts or pine nuts; ½ tsp mustard powder; 2 tsp Cranberry sauce; or a few drops of Tabasco or Worcestershire sauce.

CHRISTMAS CAKES

Part of the fun of the Christmas run-up is making the Christmas Cake. On the next few pages are a selection of traditional and novelty Christmas cakes, including two stunning cake designs from Jane Asher, the Christmas Rose Cake and the Chocolate Christmas Pudding Cake.

CHRISTMAS ROSE CAKE

This recipe makes a light cake. Use dark brown sugar for a traditional Christmas cake.

185 g (6 oz) butter
185 g (6 oz) soft light brown sugar
6 eggs, size 2
220 g (7 oz) plain flour
finely grated rind of 1 lemon and 1 orange
30 g (1 oz) mixed spice
60 g (2 oz) flaked almonds
90 g (3 oz) raisins
125 g (4 oz) sultanas
90g (3 oz) currants
60 g (2 oz) glacé cherries
60 g (2 oz) chopped mixed dried peel

DECORATION

250 g (8 oz) marzipan
2 tbsp apricot jam, boiled and sieved
cooled boiled water or sherry
750 g (1½ lb) sugarpaste
apple green petal dust
small quantity of royal icing, see page 50
small quantity of caster sugar, coloured yellow
holly green, Christmas red and pale green food colourings, plus a selection of other colours

Serves 14-16

1 Grease and line a 20 cm (8 in) round cake tin with greased greaseproof paper. Preheat oven to 150°C (300°F/Gas 2).

2 Place butter and sugar in a bowl and cream together until light and fluffy. Gradually beat in the eggs.

3 Sift flour then fold into creamed mixture. Fold in remaining ingredients.

4 Spoon cake mixture into prepared cake tin and spread evenly, making a slight dip towards the centre to allow for rising. Bake cake in oven for 2-2½ hours until firm to the touch.

5 Allow cake to cool in tin, then turn out and remove paper. Roll out marzipan on a surface lightly dusted with icing sugar to a 25 cm (10 in) round. Brush cake with apricot glaze, then cover the cake with marzipan. Trim excess marzipan from base of cake and allow to dry for a day.

6 Brush marzipanned cake with water or sherry. Roll out 500 g (1 lb) sugarpaste on a surface lightly dusted with icing sugar to a round large enough to cover the cake. Cover cake with sugarpaste and smooth top and sides. Trim excess sugarpaste from base of cake.

7 Roll out 60 g (2 oz) of the remaining sugarpaste and cut out Christmas roses using a blossom cutter. Using a rounded modelling tool or something similar press out sections gently to form petal shapes. Place petals in egg carton or apple tray to dry. Reserve trimmings.

8 When roses are dry, lightly dust centres with green petal dust. Colour a small quantity of royal icing yellow and pipe into the centres of the roses, then sprinkle with yellow sugar.

9 Colour 60 g (2 oz) of the remaining sugarpaste holly green, then roll out. Cut out holly leaves using a holly leaf cutter or sharp knife and mark veins on leaves. Reserve trimmings. Either make red berries with sugarpaste trimmings, or pipe on with red royal icing.

10 Colour 60 g (2 oz) of the remaining sugarpaste pale green. Cut a template out of card to mistletoe and ivy leaf shapes. Roll out sugarpaste and cut round templates to make leaves. Reserve trimmings. Roll berries from white sugarpaste.

11 For parcels, cut shapes from the remaining white and different coloured sugarpaste trimmings. Decorate the parcels with ribbons and bows made from sugarpaste trimmings. Finally, paint designs on the parcels, and paint the ivy leaves a darker shade of green.

12 Arrange roses, leaves, berries and parcels on cake, using a little royal icing to secure.

13 Pipe "Merry Christmas" in red icing on the top of the cake and a decorative edging on the cake board. Pipe royal icing shells around the base.

CHRISTMAS CAKES

COOK'S TIP

To cover the cake board, roll out about an extra 125 g (4 oz) sugarpaste. Roll it to a round large enough to cover the cake board. Transfer to board, trim and decorate the edge using crimpers or a fork. Position the cake in the centre of the board.

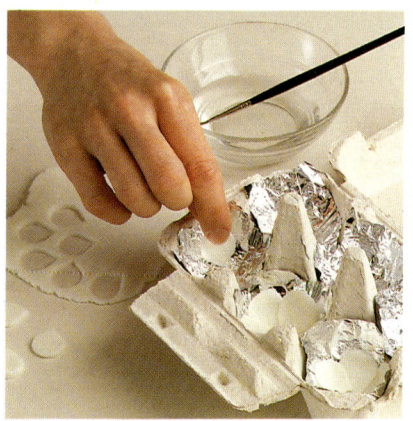

Step 7

Step 11

43

GLAZED CHRISTMAS CAKE

Topped with fruit and nuts, this cake makes the perfect alternative to a traditional iced Christmas cake.

250 g (8 oz) each sultanas, currants and raisins
125 g (4 oz) chopped dried mixed peel
250 g (8 oz) glacé cherries
60 g (2 oz) glacé pineapple
60 g (2 oz) dates
4 tbsp brandy
250 g (8 oz) butter or margarine, softened
155 g (5 oz) soft light brown sugar
5 eggs
60 g (2 oz) dark chocolate, melted and cooled
1 tsp each vanilla and almond essences
2 tsp glycerine
2 tsp raspberry jam
finely grated rind and juice of 1 lemon
250 g (8 oz) plain flour
1 tsp each mixed spice and ground ginger
¼ tsp salt
extra 2 tbsp brandy

TO DECORATE

2 tbsp apricot jam, boiled and sieved
a selection of whole nuts and red and green glacé cherries

Serves 24-30

1 Line a 20 cm (8 in) round or square tin: Cut a circle or square of greaseproof paper the size of the base of the tin, then a strip of greaseproof paper long enough to go right around the sides of the tin allowing a good overlap and about 5 cm (2 in) higher. Make slantwise cuts along one edge of this strip of paper about 3 cm (1½ in) high. Grease the tin and fit the long strip of paper inside with the snipped margin lying flat around the bottom. Fit the piece of paper for the base of the tin over this.

2 Place sultanas, currants, raisins and mixed peel in a bowl. Cut cherries, pineapple and dates into small pieces with kitchen scissors and add to the bowl. Toss fruits with brandy. Cover and set aside overnight.

3 Preheat oven to 150°C (300°F/Gas 2). Beat butter or margarine until soft and creamy. Add brown sugar and beat until light and fluffy. This will take about 5 minutes with an electric mixer. Add eggs one at a time, beating well after each addition. Stir in melted chocolate, vanilla and almond essences, glycerine, raspberry jam and finely grated lemon rind and juice.

4 Sift together flour, mixed spice, ginger and salt. Add dry ingredients to the creamed mixture alternately with the soaked fruit, ending with flour. Mix ingredients together well.

5 Spoon mixture into the prepared tin and smooth top with back of a spoon. Lift tin and allow to drop on a flat surface to break up any air bubbles. Place in oven and bake for 3-3½ hours, or until cake is firm to the touch and cooked when tested with a fine skewer.

6 Remove cake from oven. Prick surface of cake with a fine skewer and sprinkle with the extra 2 tablespoons of brandy. Cool cake in tin on a wire rack, then turn cake out of tin. Leave paper on cake, wrap in 2 thicknesses of foil and store in an airtight container.

7 When ready to decorate, brush top of cake with apricot jam and arrange nuts and cherries as shown opposite.

Step 2

Step 3

Step 4

Step 5

Christmas Cakes

BUCHE NOEL

SPONGE

60 g (2 oz) plain flour
½ tsp baking powder
¼ tsp salt
60 g (2 oz) dark chocolate, chopped
4 eggs
185 g (6 oz) caster sugar
1 tsp vanilla essence
2 tbsp warm water
¼ tsp bicarbonate of soda
icing sugar

BUTTERCREAM

185 g (6 oz) butter, softened
500 g (1 lb) icing sugar
4 tbsp cocoa powder
2-3 tbsp milk

Serves 10-12

1 Lightly grease a 30 × 25 cm (12 × 10 in) Swiss roll tin. Cut a rectangle of greaseproof paper or non-stick baking paper about 3 cm (1½ in) wider all around than the tin. Cut slits 2 cm (¾ in) long in each corner of the paper. Fit into the tin, tucking corners under so they fit neatly. If using greaseproof paper, grease lightly.

2 Preheat oven to 200°C (400°F/Gas 6). Sift flour, baking powder and salt onto a sheet of greaseproof paper and set aside. Place chocolate in a bowl set over a saucepan of simmering water and stir until melted. Set aside. Place eggs and sugar in a large mixing bowl and beat at high speed with an electric mixer for about 5 minutes, until thick and light. The mixture should be thick enough to leave a trail when beaters are lifted.

3 Add the sifted flour and vanilla essence all at once and fold in gently and quickly with a metal spoon. Add water and bicarbonate of soda to melted chocolate and stir until thick and smooth. Pour chocolate into egg and flour mixture. Fold in with a metal spoon until ingredients are just combined. Do not beat mixture.

4 Pour mixture into the prepared tin and shake gently so it reaches into the corners. Bake in oven for 15 minutes, or until cake springs back when lightly touched with fingers. Remove cake from oven and turn out onto a clean tea-towel which has been sprinkled thickly with icing sugar.

5 Peel off the lining paper and trim crisp edges of cake with a sharp knife.

Christmas Cakes

6 Fold the hem of the tea-towel over the short edge of the cake and roll up cake, using the tea-towel to help roll. Place roll on a wire rack and leave until completely cold.

7 For the buttercream, beat butter until soft and light. Sift icing sugar and cocoa into butter. Beat until mixture is smooth and creamy. Add milk and beat until combined. Carefully unroll the cake and spread quickly with half the buttercream. Roll up again.

8 Cut two 1 cm (½ in) slices on the slant from the cake and arrange on top to resemble a gnarled log. Frost entire cake with remaining buttercream and use a fork to make whorls and lines resembling bark. Chill cake until ready to serve and decorate with a sprig of holly.

Step 1

Step 2

Step 3

Step 4

Step 5

Step 6

Step 8

COOK'S TIPS

• Despite its delicate texture and creamy frosting, the cake may be frozen up to 3 weeks ahead of serving. After filling and frosting, place on a tray and freeze until hard, then wrap in freezer wrap. It will take only 30 minutes or so to thaw at room temperature.

• For a pretty effect when serving, the serving board may be sprinkled thickly with icing sugar to look like snow. Add a little Santa and other Christmas figures if you wish.

Chocolate Christmas Pudding Cake

This delicious chocolate cake makes a lovely change from traditional rich fruit cake for Christmas.

6 eggs, size 2
155 g (5 oz) butter
185 g (6 oz) caster sugar
125 g (4 oz) dark chocolate
155 g (5 oz) plain flour
1 tsp baking powder

ICING

250 g (8 oz) chocolate buttercream made with 90 g (3 oz) butter and 185 g (6 oz) icing sugar
250 g (8 oz) dark chocolate
90 ml (3 fl oz) double cream
handful of small raisins or currants
90 g (3 oz) sugarpaste

Serves 8-10

1 Grease and flour two halves of a 20 cm (8 in) diameter spherical cake mould or two 625 ml (20 fl oz) pudding basins. Preheat oven to 180°C (350°F/Gas 4).

2 Separate the eggs. Place butter and 125 g (4 oz) of the sugar in a bowl and cream together. Beat in egg yolks, one at a time.

3 Break up the chocolate, place in a heatproof bowl and melt over a saucepan of hot water. Alternatively, melt chocolate in a microwave-proof bowl in microwave on full power for 1-2 minutes. Add chocolate to sugar and egg mixture.

4 Whisk egg whites until light and fluffy, then fold in remaining sugar. Sift flour and baking powder together, then carefully fold into chocolate mixture alternating spoonfuls of flour and meringue.

5 Pour cake mixture into mould or pudding basins. Bake in two separate halves for about 30 minutes until firm to the touch.

6 Allow cakes to cool, then turn out and trim flat surfaces level. Spread halves with buttercream then join together. If using basins, trim to a round shape with a sharp serrated knife. Cover cake all over with a thin layer of buttercream. Put cake in refrigerator and allow to set for 30 minutes.

7 Meanwhile, melt the chocolate as in step 3. In a small saucepan, bring cream to boiling point, then stir into melted chocolate. Place cake on a cooling rack over a baking tray or similar to catch excess and spread chocolate mixture over the cake, scooping up excess as necessary and making sure all the cake is covered. Press a few raisins or currants into chocolate before it sets. Transfer cake to a cake board, coated in sugarpaste if liked.

8 Roll out sugarpaste on a surface lightly dusted with icing sugar, keeping back a small amount for holly. Cut 'cream shape' out of sugarpaste and press onto top of cake. Colour most of the remaining sugarpaste green and a small amount red. Roll out and cut out holly leaves out of the green sugarpaste using a cutter or sharp knife and roll small pieces of red sugarpaste with fingers to form berries. Stick leaves and berries to top of cream with water.

Step 7

Step 8

COOK'S TIP

This fun Christmas cake makes a perfect centrepiece for a party buffet table. It can be decorated up to 2 days in advance and kept in a cool place.

Christmas Cakes

ROYAL-ICED CHRISTMAS CAKE

750 g (1½ lb) mixed dried fruit
125 g (4 oz) glacé cherries, chopped
125 g (4 oz) dried apricots, chopped
90 g (3 oz) stoned prunes, chopped
60 g (2 oz) Brazil nuts, chopped
grated rind and juice of 1 lemon
3 tbsp brandy
280 g (9 oz) plain flour
2 tsp ground mixed spice
220 g (7 oz) butter, softened
60 g (2 oz) ground almonds
220 g (7 oz) soft dark brown sugar
1½ tbsp black treacle
4 eggs, beaten
750 g (1½ lb) white marzipan
3 tbsp apricot jam, boiled and sieved

ROYAL ICING

2 egg whites
2 tsp glycerine
1 tsp lemon juice
500 g (1 lb) icing sugar, sifted
ribbon to trim cake and Christmas cake decorations

Serves 24-30

1 Prepare a 20 cm (8 in) round cake tin as for Glazed Christmas Cake on page 44. Preheat oven to 140°C (275°F/Gas 1).

2 Combine dried fruit, cherries, apricots, prunes, nuts, lemon rind, juice and brandy in a bowl.

3 Mix flour, spice, butter, almonds, sugar, treacle and eggs together in a large bowl, then beat with wooden spoon for 1-2 minutes until smooth and glossy. Stir in fruit mixture.

4 Place mixture in prepared tin, smooth top and bake in oven for 3-3¼ hours, or until a fine skewer inserted into the centre of the cake comes out clean. Cool in tin. Turn cake out, remove paper and place on a 25 cm (10 in) round cake board.

5 Roll out marzipan to a 25 cm (10 in) round. Brush cake with apricot jam, then cover with marzipan. Trim excess marzipan from base of cake.

6 To make royal icing, place egg whites, glycerine and lemon juice in a bowl. Gradually beat in icing sugar until icing peaks softly. Spread icing over cake. Press a palette knife onto icing and pull away sharply to form peaks, leaving a band for the ribbon.

7 Tie ribbon around cake sides and decorate with holly leaves and a selection of Christmas decorations of your choice.

Left: *Royal-Iced Christmas Cake;*
Right: *Cranberry & Clementine Cake*

COOK'S TIPS

- *According to the consistency made, royal icing can be used to flat ice or coat the top and sides of a marzipanned cake as illustrated opposite, or used for piping. For coating the top and sides of the cake, the consistency is known as soft peak. For piping, the royal icing should be of a firmer, sharp peak consistency.*
- *When adding icing sugar to the egg white mixture, take care not to add it too quickly or this will produce a dull, heavy icing which is difficult to handle.*

CRANBERRY & CLEMENTINE CAKE

185 g (6 oz) self-raising flour
185 g (6 oz) caster sugar
185 g (6 oz) butter, softened
3 eggs, lightly beaten
60 g (2 oz) cranberries, chopped

FROSTING

2 clementines
375 g (12 oz) icing sugar, sifted
185 g (6 oz) butter, softened

TO FINISH

2 tbsp boiling water
1 tbsp caster sugar
8 cranberries and finely pared clementine rind to decorate

Serves 12

Christmas Cakes

1 Lightly grease and line two 20 cm (8 in) round sandwich tins. Preheat oven to 160°C (325°F/Gas 3).

2 Mix flour, sugar, butter and eggs in a bowl, then beat with a wooden spoon for 1-2 minutes until smooth and glossy. Stir in cranberries.

3 Divide mixture between prepared tins, smooth tops and bake in oven for 35-40 minutes or until cake springs back when lightly pressed in centre. Turn out onto a wire rack and leave until cold.

4 For frosting, grate a little clementine rind finely, squeeze 2 tbsp juice and place in a bowl with icing sugar and butter. Beat until light and fluffy. Place 4 tbsp frosting in a piping bag fitted with a small star nozzle.

5 Sandwich cakes together with a third of the frosting and spread remainder on the top and sides. Pipe a frosting lattice and border on top of cake.

6 Heat water and sugar in a small saucepan, add finely pared clementine rind and simmer for 30 seconds, then remove with a fork. Add remaining cranberries to syrup and cook gently for 30 seconds. Leave until cold. Decorate top of cake with clementine rind and cranberries.

COOK'S TIPS

- *If fresh cranberries are not available, simply substitute with an equal quantity of bottled cranberry sauce, or chopped glacé cherries.*
- *This cake can be prepared in advance and frozen without the cranberry decoration for up to 2 months. Thaw at room temperature for approximately 2 hours, then complete the decoration.*

CHRISTMAS STOLLEN

375 g (12 oz) mixed dried fruit
90 g (3 oz) blanched almonds, chopped
2 tbsp dark rum
30 g (1 oz) fresh yeast
60 ml (2 fl oz) lukewarm water
125 g (4 oz) caster sugar
625 g (1¼ lb) plain flour
250 ml (8 fl oz) lukewarm milk
2 eggs, beaten
250 g (8 oz) butter, cut into small pieces and softened
½ tsp salt
30 g (1 oz) butter, melted
beaten egg for glaze
sifted icing sugar to decorate

Serves 12

1 Combine the dried fruit, almonds and rum. Crumble yeast into a small bowl. Stir in lukewarm water and 1 teaspoon of the sugar. Stir until yeast dissolves. Set aside for 5 minutes until frothy.

2 Sift 250 g (8 oz) flour into a large bowl. Stir in yeast mixture and lukewarm milk. Cover with plastic wrap and let stand in a warm place for about 1 hour until dough has doubled in volume. Preheat oven to 190°C (375°F/Gas 5).

3 Knock down the dough firmly with fist and work in beaten eggs, remaining caster sugar and pieces of softened butter.

4 Sift remaining 375 g (12 oz) flour with salt and work in 250 g (8 oz) to dough to form a soft dough. This is easiest to do by hand. Turn out dough on a lightly floured surface and knead in enough of remaining flour to form a smooth and satiny dough without any stickiness. Work in fruit and nut mixture.

5 Divide dough in half. On a lightly floured surface, pat or roll each portion into an oval shape about 30 × 20 cm (12 × 8 in) and 2 cm (¾ in) thick. Brush each piece with melted butter and fold the dough over lengthwise, almost in half.

6 Lightly press edges together to seal and brush tops with beaten egg. Bake in oven for 35-40 minutes until well risen and golden brown. Remove from oven and brush tops again with melted butter. When cool, dust the Stollen generously with sifted icing sugar or drizzle with glacé icing and decorate with dried fruits and nuts, see below.

GLACE ICING

185 g (6 oz) icing sugar, sifted
2-3 tsp warm water, or orange or lemon juice

1 Place sifted icing sugar in a bowl and gradually add enough water, or orange or lemon juice until icing is of a consistency to coat the back of a spoon.

2 Pour icing over stollen and decorate with fruits and nuts while icing is still soft. Allow icing to set before slicing.

COOK'S TIPS

• *This quantity makes 2 Stollen. To keep them fresh, wrap securely in foil – or you can make them well ahead of time and freeze until Christmas.*
• *Stollen also make wonderful gifts for friends and they look very inviting wrapped in clear cellophane and tied with bright ribbons.*
• *The recipe calls for fresh yeast but if preferred replace with 7g (¼ oz) sachet of dried yeast instead.*

Step 1

Step 2

Step 3

Christmas Cakes

Step 4

Step 5

Step 6

53

Step 1

Step 2

Step 3

Christmas Cakes

BISHOP'S BREAD

This colourful loaf of glacé fruit, whole nuts and brandy will become a firm favourite not just at Christmas time.

2 eggs
125 g (4 oz) caster sugar
125 g (4 oz) plain flour
1 tsp baking powder
¼ tsp salt
375 g (12 oz) mixed glacé fruit such as pineapple, pears, peaches, apricots
125 g (4 oz) mixed red and green glacé cherries
375 g (12 oz) raisins
500 g (1 lb) shelled whole nuts such as almonds, Brazils, pecans or walnuts
75 ml (2½ fl oz) brandy, rum or orange liqueur
extra glacé fruits to decorate

Serves 12-14

1 Preheat oven to 150°C (300°F/Gas 2). Grease 2 loaf tins about 25 × 8 × 4cm (10 × 3 × 1½ in) and line base and sides with non-stick baking paper or greased greaseproof paper.

2 Beat eggs and sugar together in a small bowl. Sift flour, baking powder and salt into a large bowl.

3 With kitchen scissors dipped in hot water, cut the mixed glacé fruit to about the same size as the cherries.

4 Add the chopped fruit, cherries and raisins to the dry ingredients and stir well to coat with flour.

5 Stir fruit mixture and nuts into egg mixture and mix together thoroughly.

6 Turn mixture into the prepared tins, pushing it well into corners. Bake in oven for 1¼ hours until firm to the touch when pressed lightly with the fingers. Remove from oven and drizzle immediately with brandy, rum or liqueur. Cool in the tins, then wrap in foil and store in the refrigerator. When ready to serve, decorate top with extra glacé fruits.

CHERRY MADEIRA CAKE

185 g (6 oz) butter, softened
185 g (6 oz) caster sugar
3 eggs, beaten
185 g (6 oz) self-raising flour
60 g (2 oz) ground almonds
155 g (5 oz) glacé cherries, finely chopped

TO GLAZE

2 tbsp apricot jam, boiled and sieved
60 g (2 oz) glacé cherries, halved
3 glacé pineapple rings, cut into pieces

Serves 12

1 Lightly grease and line an 18cm (7 in) round cake tin. Preheat oven to 160°C (325°F/Gas 3).

2 Beat butter and sugar together in a bowl until light and fluffly. Gradually add the eggs, beating well after each addition. Sift in flour, ground almonds, chopped cherries and fold carefully into mixture.

3 Place mixture into prepared tin, smooth top and bake for 1-1¼ hours or until cake springs back when pressed in the centre. Cool in tin 5 minutes, turn out onto a wire rack, remove paper, invert cake and leave until cold.

4 Brush glaze over top of cake. Arrange halved glacé cherries and pineapple pieces on top and brush with remaining glaze.

COOK'S TIPS

- *Mixed glacé fruit really adds a special touch to a cake, and although more expensive than dried fruit it is well worth trying.*
- *Both these cakes keep well wrapped in foil and stored in an airtight container for up to two weeks. Drizzle with glacé icing, see page 52, just before serving, if liked.*

Step 4

Step 5

Step 6

THE MOST OF LEFTOVERS

Try these delicious recipes to transform leftover food from Christmas.

HAM & MUSHROOM ROLLS

8 large slices ham
185 g (6 oz) cream cheese
185 ml (6 fl oz) soured cream
1 egg, lightly beaten
1 small onion, finely chopped
125 g (4 oz) cooked spinach, well drained and chopped
pinch each of nutmeg and dry mustard
salt and pepper to taste
celery leaves to garnish

MUSHROOM SAUCE

250 ml (8 fl oz) cream of mushroom soup
60 ml (2 fl oz) soured cream

Serves 4

Step 1

Step 2

1 Preheat oven to 180°C (350°F/Gas 4). Remove any fat from ham. Combine cheese, soured cream, egg, onion, spinach and seasonings. Place about 2 tbsp of filling on each slice of ham and roll up.

2 Arrange rolls seam-side down in a shallow baking dish. Combine sauce ingredients and salt and pepper, then spoon over rolls. Bake in oven for 25 minutes. Garnish with celery leaves.

COOK'S TIPS

This recipe can be varied according to what you have left over after Christmas.
- *Turkey or pork slices make good alternatives to the ham.*
- *The cream cheese can be substituted with Danish blue or blue Stilton cheese which should be mashed well before combining with the soured cream.*
- *Other soups can also be used, such as celery or tomato.*

HAM & TURKEY NIÇOISE

750 g (1½ lb) small new potatoes
salt and pepper to taste
125 g (4 oz) French beans, topped and tailed
125 g (4 oz) cooked turkey, cut into strips
250 g (8 oz) ham, cut into strips
8 black olives
125 g (4 oz) cherry tomatoes, halved
¼ bunch spring onions, sliced diagonally
2 hard-boiled eggs, quartered

THE MOST OF LEFTOVERS

HAM AND POTATO CAKES

185 g (6 oz) ham, finely chopped
1 medium potato, cooked and mashed
1 tbsp snipped chives or
2 spring onions, chopped
freshly ground pepper to taste
60 g (2 oz) plain flour
2 tbsp vegetable oil
4 slices fresh or canned pineapple
salad leaves to serve

Serves 4

1 Combine ham, potato, chives or spring onions and pepper.

2 Shape mixture into 4 cakes and coat them lightly in flour. Heat oil in a frying pan and fry cakes on both sides until golden brown, allowing about 3 minutes each side.

3 Drain ham cakes. Serve with pineapple and salad.

Step 1

Step 2

DRESSING

75 ml (2½ fl oz) olive oil
2 tbsp red wine vinegar
½ clove garlic, crushed
1 tbsp wholegrain mustard
pinch of sugar

Serves 4

1 Cook potatoes in a saucepan of boiling salted water for 10-12 minutes until just cooked. Drain and allow to cool. Blanch beans in boiling water, then refresh in cold water and drain. Transfer potatoes and beans to a large serving bowl.

2 Add turkey, ham, olives, cherry tomatoes, spring onions and egg to the bowl.

3 To make dressing, stir all ingredients together with salt and pepper in a small bowl until combined. Pour over the salad and toss gently to mix.

Clockwise from top right: *Turkey Creole; Turkey & Chutney Loaf; Ham and Potato Cakes; Ham and Turkey Niçoise; and Ham and Mushroom Rolls.*

Three Cheese Pizza

PIZZA DOUGH

15 g (½ oz) dried yeast
125 ml (4 fl oz) warm water
500 g (1 lb) plain flour
good pinch of salt
2 tbsp olive oil

TOPPING

45 g (1½ oz) butter
2 large onions, sliced
3 tomatoes, skinned and chopped
2 tbsp chopped basil or marjoram
125 g (4 oz) blue Stilton cheese, crumbled
125 g (4 oz) mozzarella cheese, sliced
125 g (4 oz) red Leicester or Cheddar cheese, grated

Serves 6

1 To prepare dough, dissolve the yeast in the water in a cup. Sift the flour and salt into a bowl, then stir in the oil and yeast liquid, adding a little extra water if necessary to give a smooth dough. Knead well, then divide in half and roll into two 20 cm (8 in) circles. Place on oiled baking sheets, cover loosely with plastic wrap and leave to rise in a warm place for 20 minutes.

2 Meanwhile, preheat oven to 200°C (400°F/Gas 6). Melt the butter in a large frying pan, add the onions and cook gently for 10 minutes.

3 Divide the tomatoes and the onion mixture between the two pizza bases. Sprinkle each with basil or marjoram. Arrange cheese on top and bake in oven for 25-30 minutes.

Stilton & Watercress Tart

PASTRY

250 g (8 oz) plain flour
pinch of salt
125 g (4 oz) butter or margarine
about 3 tbsp cold water

FILLING

30 g (1 oz) butter
2 bunches watercress, stalks removed
315 g (10 oz) blue Stilton cheese, rind removed and diced
3 eggs
155 ml (5 fl oz) single cream
salt and pepper to taste
salad leaves and radishes to serve

Serves 4

1 Preheat oven to 200°C (400°F/Gas 6). To make pastry, sift flour and salt into a large bowl. Rub in butter or margarine until the mixture resembles breadcrumbs. Add the water and mix to a firm dough.

2 Roll out pastry on a lightly floured surface and use to line an oiled 20 cm (8 in) flan tin. Prick base and chill for 15 minutes, then bake blind in oven for 10-12 minutes. Lower oven temperature to 180°C (350°F/Gas 4).

3 Meanwhile prepare filling. Melt butter in a large frying pan, add the watercress and cook for 1-2 minutes, stirring constantly, until just wilted. Drain in sieve, pressing out excess liquid, then arrange in the pastry case. Tuck the Stilton cubes into the watercress.

4 Beat together eggs and cream, season with salt and pepper and pour into the flan case. Bake for 30-35 minutes or until set. Serve warm or cold with salad leaves and chives.

Turkey & Chutney Loaf

Illustrated on page 56

375g (12 oz) cooked turkey, finely chopped
90 g (3 oz) fresh white breadcrumbs
2 eggs
1 small onion, chopped
2 tbsp chutney
90 ml (3 fl oz) milk
2-3 tsp ground paprika
4 tbsp finely chopped parsley
cherry tomatoes and salad leaves to serve

Serves 6

1 Preheat oven to 180°C (350°F/Gas 4). Place all ingredients in a large bowl and mix well.

2 Press mixture into a greased 500 g (1 lb) loaf tin and bake in oven for 35-40 minutes. Serve loaf sliced, hot or cold with tomatoes and salad leaves.

COOK'S TIPS

- *If preferred, replace the cooked turkey with an equal quantity of cooked lean ham.*
- *This loaf is delicious served hot with a spicy tomato sauce.*

Left: *Stilton and Watercress Tart*; Right: *Three Cheese Pizza*

TURKEY CREOLE

Illustrated on page 56

15 g (½ oz) butter
1 clove garlic, crushed
1 small onion, finely chopped
1 tbsp plain flour
1 tsp chilli powder
155 ml (5 fl oz) tomato juice
155 ml (5 fl oz) chicken stock
375 g (12 oz) cooked turkey, chopped
125 g (4 oz) button mushrooms, sliced
salt and pepper to taste
boiled rice to serve
cayenne pepper and bay leaves to garnish

Serves 4

1 Melt butter in a medium saucepan and sauté garlic and onion until softened. Stir in flour and chilli powder and cook for 1 minute, stirring.

2 Gradually add tomato juice and chicken stock to pan. Bring slowly to the boil and simmer until sauce thickens, stirring constantly.

3 Stir turkey, mushrooms and salt and pepper to taste into sauce. Bring to the boil for 5 minutes, then simmer for 2 minutes. Serve with boiled rice, sprinkled with cayenne pepper and garnished with bay leaves.

FESTIVE CHEER

Christmas is the perfect opportunity to let out the stops and indulge in wines you would otherwise not normally try. Here, Andrew Jefford, a leading wine writer, offers advice on Champagne and sparkling wine alternatives, wines to complement the Christmas menu plus after-dinner tipples. There is also a section on cocktails, including non-alcoholic versions, to get you into the Christmas spirit.

CHAMPAGNE & SPARKLING WINES

The pop of a cork is synonymous with the opening of every festivity, and there is no better way to wake the palate up for the festive treats that lie ahead than with a crisp sparkling wine. Champagne, at its best, is peerless: it has the finest foam, the headiest scent, the most complex and elegant flavour of all sparkling wines. Not all Champagne, unfortunately, is of exceptional quality, so choose carefully: the best of the large champagne houses (such as Pol Roger, Roederer or Taittinger) produce reliably good wines, while supermarket 'own-label' and growers' Champagnes can be good value.

Alternatives to Champagne are numerous and increasingly high in quality, with California (e.g. Mumm's Cuvée Napa) and New Zealand (e.g. Deutz's Marlborough Cuvée, Montana's Lindauer) leading the way in terms of finesse. Australian sparkling wines (such as those in the Seppelt's Great Western range) are sound and solid, as is Cava from Spain. If you prefer a sweeter sparkling wine, the Italian Moscato d'Asti is irresistably perfumed and grapey, and has the added virtue of being low in alcohol.

WINES FOR THE CHRISTMAS MEAL

Wine lovers have much to thank the turkey for, since it is a meat that can be happily partnered by either a light or a full white wine, or a medium-bodied red wine. White wines for Burgundy are perfect choices: if you like something light, and very dry, try Aligoté; for a fuller match, choose a good Mâcon-Villages. If you can afford to splash out, the best white Burgundies from the Côte d'Or (such as Meursault or Puligny-Montrachet, better still a Premier Cru wine from one of these villages) make superb Christmas lunch whites. For a sweeter touch, choose a German Kabinett or Spätlese wine from the Mosel or Rheingau.

The best reds for turkey are soft, rich and ripe: Christmas lunch is a good moment to try a Beaujolais cru wine (such as Fleurie or Juliénas), a Côtes-du-Rhône-Villages, or wines from California or Chile based on the Merlot grape variety (stated on label). Australian Shiraz wines combine softness with beefiness, and make a richer but no less memorable match. If you are addicted to claret, the Christmas turkey will generally get on better with a Saint-Emilion or Pomerol wine (in which Merlot is predominant) than with a wine from the Médoc (where Cabernet Sauvignon has the upper hand).

If goose is your Christmas choice, on the other hand, then a claret from the Médoc is ideal; so, too, would be lively Cabernet Sauvignon wines from Australia or California, a good Chianti from Tuscany, or a Barolo or Barbaresco from Northern Italy. Duck is delicious with lively white wines containing both acidity and a little sweetness: Vouvray from the Loire valley is very good, and so are Halbtrocken Kabinett or Spätlese wines from the Rheingau, Rheinpfalz, Rheinhessen and Nahe.

Christmas pudding throws out a challenge that few wines are able to meet: Bual or Malmsey Madeira, or fortified Muscat wines such as Muscat de Beaumes-de-Venise or the Spanish Moscatel de Valencia, match the pud weight for weight, but a surprisingly good contrast is achieved by the sparkling Moscato d'Asti.

AND TO FINISH...

Save Port for the cheese. This is the great moment of the year to serve Vintage Port; less expensive choices are provided by Crusting Port (which, like Vintage, requires decanting) or Late Bottled Vintage Port (which does not generally need decanting). A 20-year-old Tawny Port, or a Colheita Port (vintage-dated Tawny), make lighter, silkier alternatives.

Alternatively you may prefer to relax over a glass of Cognac. The slightly more fiery Armagnac is perhaps best kept for another occasion (it makes a reviving warmer after an evening's carol singing); Calvados, by contrast, with its subtle apple flavour, follows the dried-fruit theme of Christmas pudding and mince pies perfectly. If you prefer whisky, a single malt aged in sherry casks, such as the Macallan, Aberlour, or the sherry-cask-aged version of Glendronach, chimes best with Christmas indulgence.

COCKTAILS

Christmas is an ideal time to experiment mixing both alcoholic and non-alcoholic cocktails. Here is an **A-Z** guide of the most popular ingredients.

Amaretto An Italian almond and apricot based liqueur

Angostura Bitters An infusion of aromatics from the West Indies, used very sparingly for flavouring.

Benedictine A sweet, golden coloured, brandy based liqueur flavoured with mixed herbs and originally made by Benedictine monks in France.

Campari Bitters A strong, bitter Italian aperitif.

Cointreau A sweet, colourless orange flavoured liqueur from France.

Crème de Banane A strong, banana flavoured liqueur.

Crème de Cacao A very sweet, brandy based liqueur made from cocoa beans. It has a cocoa-vanilla flavour and is chocolate brown in colour.

Crème de Cassis A brandy based liqueur, flavoured with blackcurrants, originally from France.

Crème de Menthe A peppermint flavoured liqueur, which can be green, white or pink.

Curaçao A sweet liqueur, which can be blue, white or orange. Made from the peel of oranges. Originally from the West Indies.

Drambuie A scotch whisky based liqueur, flavoured with herbs and honey.

Fraise Liqueur Strawberry flavoured liqueur.

Galliano An Italian, golden coloured liqueur, flavoured with liquorice and aniseed.

Grenadine A French non-alcoholic fruit syrup made from pomegranates with a slight redcurrant flavour.

Kahlua Made from Mexican coffee beans.

Kummel Caraway flavoured liqueur.

Malibu A coconut and rum spirit.

Marashino Made from Maraschino cherries and their crushed kernels.

Tequila A clear spirit distilled in Mexico from a cactus-like plant.

Tia Maria A Jamaican rum based liqueur with coffee and spices.

TROPICAL CUP

1 ripe mango, peeled and sliced
1 small melon, peeled and roughly chopped
90 g (3 oz) caster sugar
juice of 1 lemon
pulp of 4 passionfruit
500 ml (16 fl oz) orange juice
1.25 litres (3 pints) chilled soda water
slices of kiwi fruit and ice cubes

Makes about 2.5 litres (4 pints)

1 Pureé mango and melon in a food processor, or push through a sieve.

2 Combine pureé with caster sugar and lemon juice. Cover and chill overnight.

3 Stir in passionfruit pulp, orange juice and chilled soda water. Decorate with slices of kiwi fruit and ice cubes.

CHAMPAGNE CUP

75 ml (2½ fl oz) brandy
75 ml (2½ fl oz) Cointreau
1 tsp angostura bitters
1 tbsp caster sugar
500 ml (16 fl oz) grape juice
2 bottles chilled Champagne or dry sparkling wine
ice cubes and small bunches of cherries or grapes

Makes 2.5 litres (4 pints)

1 Combine brandy, Cointreau, bitters, caster sugar and grape juice. Cover and chill overnight.

2 Pour into a large jug or punch bowl and stir in Champagne or sparkling wine.

3 Add ice cubes and decorate edges of jug or punch bowl with cherries or grapes.

MIXER'S TIPS

- *It is usual to stir clear drinks and shake or blend drinks which contain fruit juice, egg white or cream.*
- *Serve cocktails as soon as they are mixed otherwise the drink could separate or become diluted by the ice.*

STRAWBERRY CUP

2 punnets of strawberries, hulled and sliced
90 g (3 oz) caster sugar
500 ml (16 fl oz) orange juice
juice of 2 lemons
1 litre (32 fl oz) chilled rosé wine
1.25 litres (3 pints) chilled bottled soda water
whole strawberries and orange and lemon slices

Makes about 2.5 litres (4 pints)

1 Combine the strawberries with caster sugar, orange and lemon juice. Cover and chill overnight.

2 Pour into a punch bowl and stir in wine and soda water. Decorate with strawberries and orange and lemon slices.

MULLED WINE

250 ml (8 fl oz) water
1 cinnamon stick
6 cloves
6 allspice berries
1 bottle red wine
185 ml (6 fl oz) port
1 tbsp caster sugar
peel of ½ lemon, cut into slices
slices of lemon

Makes about 1 litre (1¾ pints)

1 Simmer water and spices in a saucepan for 20 minutes.

2 Pour red wine into another saucepan. Strain in spiced water. Reserve spices for garnish.

3 Add port and sugar to pan and heat until mixture is almost boiling. Serve hot with lemon peel and slices. Garnish with reserved spices.

PEACH CUP

400 g (14 oz) canned peaches in natural juice
125 g (4 oz) caster sugar
500 ml (16 fl oz) peach juice
juice of 1 lemon
1.25 litres (3 pints) chilled lemonade
peach and lemon slices

Makes about 2 litres (3¼ pints)

1 Chop peaches very finely and place in a bowl with caster sugar, peach juice and lemon juice. Cover and chill.

2 Transfer to a punch bowl and stir in lemonade. Decorate with peach and lemon slices.

Above: *Mulled Wine*

TABLE DECORATIONS

With the Christmas menu planned, now spare a thought to the little extra finishing touches that will make this a Christmas to remember.

APPLES & NIGHTLIGHTS

If this arrangement is too big for your dining table; it could be placed on a side table.

YOU WILL NEED:

soaked green oasis
large, low flat dish
wire netting
silver reel wire
plenty of pine
10 nightlights
at least 20 red apples
1.25 mm (18 gauge) stub wires

1 Place oasis in dish, then trim off the corners with a sharp kitchen knife to make a mound shape. Cover with wire netting, securing it to the dish with silver reel wire.

2 Strip the lower needles from the pine twigs, about 15 cm (6 in) long, then arrange them in oasis at an angle of 45° until it has been completely covered.

3 With a thin-bladed knife, cut a hole big enough to take a nightlight in the top of ten of the apples. Place an unlit nightlight into each hole. Wire the apples by pushing a stub wire into the base and out the other side. Arrange all the apples in the oasis, securing in place with the stub wires.

4 Light the nightlights half an hour before the guests are due, but take care that no pine is overhanging the candles as this could become a fire hazard.

Step 3

WIRING DECORATIONS

To make the following garlands, rings and table centres, you will need to use wired decorations. Here are the basic steps to wiring cones, nuts and pine.

To wire cones, for use in arrangements use 1.25 mm (18 gauge) stub wires unless cones are very small, in which case 0.71 mm (22 gauge) wires should be used. Loop the wire through the bottom kernels of the cone and twist tightly and securely on to itself.

For walnuts, dip one end of 1.25 mm (18 gauge) stub wire into an all-purpose glue and then stick it up the bottom of the nut. For harder nuts, such as Brazil nuts, you will have to drill a small hole before inserting the wire.

To wire pine, first strip off the bottom needles, then turn one end of a stub wire back and lay the flattened loop against the stem. Twist the longer end around the wire and stem, as shown.

NAPKIN GARLANDS

Napkin garlands can be made from virtually anything but each item must be wired individually and the stems covered with the green floristry tape.

YOU WILL NEED:

napkins
1.25 mm (18 gauge) stub wire
green floristry tape
silver-sprayed pine cones,
walnuts and pine tips

1 Wire the cones, walnuts and pine stems, *see left*.

2 Measure three-quarters of the circumference of the napkin when rolled up, using stub wire, and cut to that length. Cover the length of wire with floristry tape and then shape it to fit the rolled-up napkin.

3 Carefully slide wire off the napkin, then wire in pine cones, walnuts and pine, or decorations of your choice.

GOLDEN ADVENT RING

A rich decoration guaranteed to enhance the festive table.

YOU WILL NEED:

green oasis ring and base
4 candle holders
golden cherubs
1.25 mm (18 gauge) stub wire
7.5-10 cm (3-4 in) long pine stems
4 gold candles
wired grapes, cones, chestnuts, walnuts and brown bows

1 Soak the oasis ring by turning it upside down in a basin of water and leaving for 10 minutes.

2 Space the candle holders around the soaked oasis ring.

3 Wire the cherubs from the back, and arrange them around the oasis ring.

4 Strip the needles from the bottom 2.5 cm (1 in) of the pine stems. Push pine tips into the

TABLE DECORATIONS

ring at an angle of about 45° until the oasis is completely covered. Then add candles still in their plastic wrappings as these will help to protect the candles from any damage while the arrangement is being made.

5 Finally, arrange wired grapes, cones, nuts and bows, to complete the ring. Remove plastic wrappings from the candles.

Step 4

Step 5

Above: *Golden Advent Ring;* and below: *Holly & Nut Table Decoration.*

HOLLY & NUT TABLE DECORATION

A simple decoration of pine, holly, walnuts and pine cones. The oval shape of this decoration is a good alternative to a round advent ring making it an ideal choice for rectangular tables.

YOU WILL NEED:

**block of soaked green oasis
black oasis tray
2 candle holders
green oasis tape
2 red candles
pine, holly, wired pine cones
and nuts,** *see left*

1 Place oasis on tray. Insert candle holders into the top of the oasis, then tape the block of oasis to the tray, as though it were a parcel, using oasis tape.

2 Put candles in their holders, but do not remove their plastic wrappings yet to protect the candles.

3 Take the tips off the blue pine and strip the needles from the lower part of each small branch. Cover the top and sides of the oasis block in pine until it is hidden.

4 Strip lower leaves from the holly, and arrange in the oasis. Add wired cones, and then wired nuts to complete the decoration. Remove plastic wrappings from candles.

Quick Reference Guide

Useful information on preparing and cooking Christmas meats and poultry, plus an invaluable food storage guide.

Turkey

THAWING

Frozen turkey must be thoroughly thawed before cooking to avoid the risk of salmonella food poisoning. Allow the bird to thaw in its bag in a cool place, preferably below 15°C (60°F) using the chart below as a guide. Obviously, the lower the room temperature the longer it will take to thaw. Do not thaw the bird in the refrigerator or in hot water. Remove the giblets and neck from the body cavity as soon as they are loose and set aside to make the gravy. When thawed, the legs will be flexible and there will be no trace of ice crystals in the body cavity. Wash the inside of the turkey thoroughly under cold running water, then pat dry with absorbent kitchen paper. If not cooking the turkey immediately wrap loosely with plastic wrap and store in the bottom of the refrigerator away from other foods for up to 2 days.

Thawing & Serving Chart

Oven-Ready Weight	Number of Servings	Thawing Time
1.5-2.5 Kg (3-5 lb)	4-6	20 hours
3-3.5 Kg (6-7 lb)	7-9	30 hours
4-4.5 Kg (8-9 lb)	10-14	36 hours
5-5.5 Kg (10-11 lb)	15-16	45 hours
6-6.5 Kg (12-13 lb)	17-18	48 hours
7-8.5 Kg (14-17 lb)	19-25	48 hours
9-11 Kg (18-22 lb)	26-37	48 hours
13 Kg (23 lb plus)	38 plus	48 hours

* Times based on thawing the bird at 15°C (60°F)

Stuffing the Bird

Before stuffing the turkey make sure the stuffing is completely cold. Only stuff the neck cavity of the bird to ensure the heat penetrates the centre and cooks the meat quickly and thoroughly. Take care not to pack the stuffing too tightly or the skin may split during cooking. Any extra stuffing may be shaped into small balls and placed in an ovenproof dish and cooked separately. A cut apple and peeled onion placed inside the clean body cavity also adds extra flavour. The stuffing may be prepared a day in advance and kept covered in the refrigerator until the bird is ready for the oven. Allow about 250 g (8 oz) prepared stuffing per 2.5 kg (5 lb) dressed weight of turkey.

Trussing the Turkey

After the bird has been stuffed, it should be trussed in order to help it retain a good shape whilst cooking.

1 Place the turkey breast-side down. Pull the loose neck skin over the neck cavity and tuck wingtips under. Secure neck skin with a metal skewer, securing wingtips to the body at the same time.

2 To secure the upper drumsticks, turn the turkey breast-side up. Thread a trussing needle with fine string and pass it through the upper part of one drumstick, then the body, and through the other drumstick. Remove needle and pull string so a length of string is protruding from both drumsticks.

3 To secure the lower drumsticks, turn turkey over and cross string over its back. Turn turkey again so it is once more breast-side up. Cross the ends of the string and tie drumsticks and 'parson's nose' together with a secure knot.

4 Place turkey breast-side up in a large roasting pan ready to cook.

ROASTING THE TURKEY

When calculating the cooking time, always use the oven-ready weight, i.e. the bird after stuffing and time the bird to be ready 15 minutes before carving. This helps ensure the flesh firms up and makes carving easier.

Place the bird in a roasting pan, and unless self-basting, brush the surface with melted butter and season with salt and pepper. The breast of the bird may also be covered with bacon rashers to help keep the flesh moist.

Alternatively, the turkey may be wrapped in foil or butter-soaked muslin. This reduces the need for basting during cooking.

Roast the bird at 190°C (375°F/Gas 5) according to the chart below. To test the bird is cooked, pierce the thickest part of both thighs with a metal skewer. When cooked, the juices should run clear with no trace of pink.

Remove bacon, foil or muslin 30 minutes before end of the recommended cooking time to allow the skin to become crisp and golden.

ROASTING CHART

Oven-Ready Weight	Without Foil	Wrapped in Foil
1.5-2.5 Kg (3-5 lb)	1½-1¾ hours	1¾-2 hours
3-3.5 Kg (6-7 lb)	1¾-2 hours	2-2¼ hours
4-4.5 Kg (8-9 lb)	2-2½ hours	2½-2¾ hours
5-5.5 Kg (10-11 lb)	2¼-2¾ hours	2½-3 hours
6-6.5 Kg (12-13 lb)	2¾-3 hours	3-3¼ hours
7-8.5 Kg (14-17 lb)	3¼-3½ hours	3½-3¾ hours
9-11 Kg (18-22 lb)	3½-3¾ hours	3¾-4 hours
13 Kg (23 lb plus)	3¾ hours plus	4¼ hours plus

* *Times based on roasting at 190°C (375°F/Gas 5)*

CARVING THE TURKEY

1 Removing the first leg. Choose a pointed knife with a very sharp edge and a long, flexible blade. Remove string and skewers from bird and place breast-side up on a carving board or plate. Hold the bird steady with a large carving fork. Cut the skin between thigh and breast. Separate the leg from the body of the turkey by bending the thigh outwards to locate the hip joint, slice down through the joint to remove the leg.

2 Separating the thigh from the drumstick. Hold the knife at an angle between the thigh and drumstick bones and cut firmly through the joint to separate the leg into two serving portions.

3 Slicing the drumstick. Cut a thick slice of meat and skin from each side of the drumstick, keeping the knife close to the bone. Cut these into smaller slices.

4 Slicing the thigh. Hold the thigh steady with a fork and slice into 4 or more pieces, depending on the size of the thigh. Repeat steps 1 to 4 with the other side of the turkey.

5 Removing a wing. Slice down through the corner of the breast toward the wing. Push the wing out to show the joint and cut through joint. Remove wing with a piece of breast attached.

6 Carving the breast. Hold the breast steady with the carving fork and slice down through the meat. When one side is carved, remove other wing and carve remaining breast meat.

STORING & REHEATING LEFTOVER TURKEY

Leftover turkey should be cooled, covered with plastic wrap or foil and refrigerated as soon as possible after cooking. Leftover stuffing should be removed from the bird and stored in a separate dish in the refrigerator. Cooked turkey should be eaten within 2 days or it can be frozen for up to 2 months, even if the bird was originally frozen. Drumsticks, wings and thighs can be frozen on the bone, or the meat can be diced or sliced for convenience ready to add a sauce for reheating. Wrap the cold turkey meat in foil or freezer wrap and label. Allow to thaw thoroughly at room temperature. When reheating cooked turkey meat, make sure it boils for at least 5 minutes and that the meat is piping hot all the way through. Do not reheat cooked turkey more than once, or refreeze it.

MAKING TURKEY STOCK

A good flavoursome turkey stock makes an excellent basis for soups and casseroles, and can be incorporated into the recipes for leftovers on page 56.

To make the stock, place turkey carcass and bones in a large saucepan. Add 1 sliced onion, a sprig of fresh thyme or bouquet garni, 2 sticks of chopped celery and 4 cloves. Cover with cold water, bring to the boil, then simmer for 1½ hours. Or to cut down on cooking time, cook in a pressure cooker at high pressure for 30 minutes. Strain, and skim fat.

Ideally stock should be made and used on the same day. If, however, stock is not required for immediate use, cool and store in the refrigerator for up to 2 days. Stock may be frozen for up to 2 months: Boil the prepared stock over a high heat to reduce by half. Cool concentrated stock, then pour into ice cube trays, and freeze until solid. Transfer to plastic bags and label. Alternatively, pour stock into 315 ml (10 fl oz) or 625 ml (20 fl oz) containers allowing about 2.5 cm (1 in) headroom as the stock will expand on freezing.

To use frozen stock cubes, thaw at room temperature, or simply add to saucepan and heat gently, stirring occasionally. Add 2tbsp water to every concentrated stock cube.

ROASTING MEAT

When purchasing a joint for roasting, allow 125-185 g (4-6 oz) per person for a boned and rolled joint, or 250-375 g (8-12 oz) per person on the bone. If cooking frozen meat it should be thoroughly thawed before cooking.

Weigh the joint in order to calculate the cooking time, then place on a trivet in a roasting pan so that the largest cut surfaces are exposed and any fat is on the top to baste the joint. Roast in the centre of a preheated oven for calculated cooking time. Once cooked, allow the joint to stand for 10 minutes before carving.

BEEF

Beef is a popular alternative to turkey at Christmas time. The best joints for roasting include sirloin, the rib joints, thick flank and whole fillet. Roast the joint according to the

ALTERNATIVES TO TURKEY

MEAT ROASTING CHART

Meat	Cooking time at 180°C (350°F/Gas 4) for bone in and boneless joints	Recommended meat thermometer internal temperatures
Beef	Rare: 20 minutes per 500 g (1 lb), plus 20 minutes extra	60°C (140°F)
	Medium: 25 minutes per 500g (1 lb), plus 25 minutes extra	70°C (160°F)
	Well done: 30 minutes per 500 g (1 lb), plus 30 minutes extra	80°C (175°F)
Pork	Medium: 30 minutes per 500 g (1 lb), plus 30 minutes extra	75-80°C (170-175°F)
	Well done: 35 minutes per 500g (1 lb), plus 35 minutes extra	80-85°C (175-185°F)
Lamb	Medium: 25 minutes per 500g (1 lb), plus 25 minutes extra	70-75°C (160-170°F)
	Well done: 30 minutes per 500 g (1 lb), plus 30 minutes extra	75-80°C (170-175°F)

When roasting stuffed joints, weigh the joint with stuffing to calculate cooking time.

timings given on the Meat Roasting Chart above, basting the meat with pan juices or red wine during cooking. If liked, rub the joint with horseradish sauce or mustard about 20 minutes before the end of recommended cooking time. Or for a delicious alternative to a plain roasted joint, press a mixture of fresh breadcrumbs, herbs and seasoning over the surface of the joint 30 minutes before the end of the cooking time.

PORK

Roast pork is traditionally served over the festive period, hot or cold as part of a cold meat platter. Leg, loin and shoulder make good roasting joints and are traditionally served with sage and onion stuffing and apple sauce, or Cumberland Sauce, see page 13. The joint is also delicious brushed with a mixture of honey and orange 20 minutes before the end of the cooking time. Alternatively, if you prefer crackling, score the rind of the joint and dry well, then brush with oil and rub in a little salt. Do not baste the joint during cooking.

LAMB

Lamb makes a refreshing change to the more traditional meats over the Christmas period. A Crown Roast or Guard of Honour makes an impressive centrepiece to the table, but whole legs and shoulders are most popular served with mint sauce or redcurrant jelly. These joints are usually sold on the bone but may also be purchased boned ready for stuffing; a mixture of chopped onion, garlic, apricots, nuts and orange rind and juice combined with fresh breadcrumbs or cooked rice makes a delicious stuffing. Alternatively the joint may be spiked with fresh rosemary or slivers of garlic, or brushed with a honey and citrus-flavoured glaze 20 minutes before the end of the recommended cooking time.

BACON & GAMMON

Bacon and gammon joints are traditionally served cold as part of a cold meat platter. Suitable joints include collar, forehock and prime back. Always check when purchasing the joint whether it needs soaking before cooking to remove excess saltiness. When advised to soak the joint, place in a saucepan of cold water and bring to the boil. Drain the water and cover with fresh water ready for cooking. Bring the water to the boil, then reduce heat and simmer for 20 minutes per 500 g (1 lb), plus an extra 20 minutes, keeping pan topped up with boiling water. For cooked joints which are to be glazed and baked, allow 10 minutes boiling time per 500 g (1 lb), plus 10 minutes extra, then bake in an oven preheated to 220°C (425°F/Gas 7) for 10 minutes per 500 g (1 lb), plus an extra 10 minutes. For joints over 5 kg (10 lb) allow 20 minutes cooking time per 500 g (1 lb). See the recipe for Honey-Glazed Ham on page 15.

CHICKEN & POUSSIN

For small gatherings over the Christmas period, a chicken or poussin makes an excellent choice. Allow a 1.75 kg (3½ lb) chicken for 3-4 persons, or one poussin per person. Roast the bird in an oven preheated to 190°C (375°F/Gas 5) allowing 20 minutes per 500 g (1 lb), plus an extra 20 minutes for a chicken, or a total cooking time of 45-50 minutes for a poussin. Brush with breast with melted butter before cooking or loosen the breast skin and rub a mixture of garlic- or mustard-flavoured butter over the flesh, taking care not to pierce the skin or the butter will ooze out during cooking. Or, brush with a honey and herb glaze 20 minutes before the end of the cooking.

DUCK

Duck makes a pleasant change to other poultry but it is a fatty bird and does not need to be brushed with melted butter before roasting; the skin must be pricked before cooking to allow the fat to run out. Sprinkle the duck with salt and pepper and roast on a trivet in a roasting pan in an oven preheated to 200°C (400°F/Gas 6) for 20 minutes per 500 g (1 lb). Allow 500 g (1 lb) meat per person and serve with Orange Sauce, see page 17, or Honey Apple Sauce, see page 13.

GOOSE

Goose is becoming an increasingly popular alternative to turkey at Christmas time. It is a rich meat and unlike turkey does not have to be brushed with melted butter before roasting. Stuff the neck cavity only and place any fat taken from its inside on top of the bird. Cover the bird loosely with foil and roast in an oven preheated to 180°C (350°F/Gas 4) allowing 25 minutes per 500 g (1 lb). Allow 375 g (12 oz) meat per person and serve with Honey Apple Sauce, or Spicy Cranberry Sauce, see page 13.

Food Storage Guide

For storage purposes, foods are divided into the following categories:

- Non-perishable products may last for 12 months or more without deterioration, if stored correctly.
- Perishable foods, when stored correctly, will keep for some time, usually up to 3 months.
- Highly perishable foods should be consumed within two to five days of purchase. See packaging for recommended storage time.
- Frozen products should keep for one to six months depending on the type of food.

Non-Perishable Foods

Canned foods Store in a cool, dry place. Avoid 'blown' or damaged cans.

Bottled foods Store in a cold, dark place.

Cereal products Store in clean, dry, airtight containers.

Perishable Foods

Bacon Wrap loosely and store in refrigerator.

Butter and margarine Refrigerate in sealable containers as these foods absorb other flavours.

Cakes and biscuits Store separately in clean, airtight containers.

Cheese Wrap loosely with greaseproof paper or foil and store in refrigerator.

Coffee When ground, place in an airtight container and store in the refrigerator.

Eggs Store carton in refrigerator.

Breakfast cereals Place in clean, airtight containers or tightly reseal packet.

Tea Store in an airtight container.

Onions and potatoes Store in a cool, dark, well-ventilated place.

Root vegetables, pears, apples Keep in refrigerator or cool, dark place.

Highly Perishable Foods

Meat and fresh poultry Loosely cover with greaseproof paper and place in the meat compartment or the coldest part of the refrigerator away from cooked foods or dairy produce such as milk or cheese.

Fresh fish Place scaled and cleaned fish in an airtight container and refrigerate for one to two days. Fish may be stored for longer periods in the freezer.

Soft fruits (except bananas) and salad vegetables May be stored in the salad compartment in the refrigerator. Melons, strawberries and pineapple should be placed in sealed containers to prevent their flavours penetrating other foods.

Milk and cream Wipe containers before placing in the refrigerator. Follow packaging instructions regarding storage times.

Bread Leave in plastic wrapper or store in breadbin which must be cleaned and aired frequently. Bread may also be stored in the freezer and slices taken out as needed.

Freezing Guide

Store manufactured frozen foods following the instructions on the packages. Most frozen foods should be thawed before cooking and serving.

How to Freeze

Cakes and desserts Seal in plastic wrap or foil. Before serving, place on a wire cake rack and thaw out completely.

Fruit and vegetables Blanch, refresh in cold water, drain thoroughly on absorbent paper and place in airtight containers or freezer bags.

Fish Clean and scale fish, seal in plastic wrap, foil or freezer bags.

Poultry Seal completely. Must be thoroughly thawed before cooking.

Meat Prepare meat for pies and casseroles before freezing. All meat should be placed in airtight containers or freezer bags. Thaw before cooking.

INDEX

A
Almonds
  almond Brussels sprouts 24
  rice and nut stuffing 10
  Roquefort and almond soup 8
Apples
  apple and hazelnut stuffing 13
  honey apple sauce 13
Apples and nightlights 63
Apricots
  apricot and orange relish 15
  apricot sherry trifle 35
Asparagus
  ham and asparagus gratins 6
Avocado
  crispy bacon and avocado salad 6

B
Bacon
  bacon-wrapped sausages 12
  crispy bacon and avocado salad 6
  serving 69
Beans with tomatoes 24
Beef
  roast fillet of beef with port and nut stuffing 18
  roasting 68
Biscuits
  Christmas tree biscuits 40
Brandy
  clear brandy sauce 37
  orange and brandy butter 37
Bread sauce 13
Broccoli
  citrus broccoli and cauliflower 22
Brussels sprouts, almond 24

C
Carrots and celery 25
Cauliflower
  cauliflower and cress soup 8
  citrus broccoli and cauliflower 22
Celery, carrots and 25
Celery with bay and bacon 24
Cheese
  cheese-pecan crisps 41
  cheese stuffing 16
  leek and stilton soufflé 4
  smoked salmon parcels 6
  stilton and watercress tart 58
  three cheese pizza 58
  Roquefort and almond soup 8
Cherries
  cherry chutney 13
  cherry Madeira cake 55
Chestnuts
  chestnut and cranberry soup 7
  chestnut bavarois 31

Chicken
  serving 69
  French roast chicken with cream gravy 16
Chicken liver mousse 8
Chocolate
  buche Noel 46
  chocolate truffles 38
  chocolate Christmas pudding cake 48
  crunchy chocolate slice 32
Christmas cakes
  bishop's bread 55
  buche Noel 46
  cherry Madeira cake 55
  chocolate Christmas pudding cake 48
  cranberry and clementine cake 50
  glazed Christmas cake 44
  royal iced Christmas cake 50
  Christmas rose cake 42
  Christmas stollen 52
Christmas puddings
  easy Christmas pudding 28
  iced Christmas pudding 35
  traditional Christmas pudding 26
Chutney
  cherry chutney 13
  turkey and chutney loaf 58
Cranberries
  chestnut and cranberry soup 7
  cranberry and clementine cake 50
  spicy cranberry sauce 13
Crudités with garlic dip 6
Cumberland sauce 13

D
Drinks
  cocktails 61, 62
  mulled wine 62
  peach cup 62
  strawberry cup 62
  tropical cup 61
  wines 60
  Champagne cup 61
Duck
  duck with orange sauce 17
  serving 69

E
Egg custard 37

F
Filo pastry
  mushroom filo tartlets 8
  vegetarian filo slice 20
Food storage 70
Fruit and nut caramels 40

G
Gammon, serving 69
Golden Advent ring 64
Goose, serving 69
Gravy
  creamy gravy 16
  perfect pan gravy 12
Green beans with Dijon mustard 24

H
Ham
  ham and asparagus gratins 6
  ham and mushroom rolls 56
  ham and potato cakes 57
  ham and turkey Niçoise 56
  honey-glazed ham 15
  melon and Parma ham 8
Hazelnuts
  apple and hazelnut stuffing 13
Holly and nut table decoration 65

L
Lamb, serving 69
Leeks
  crispy leeks 25
  leek and stilton soufflé 4
Lemon mousse 31

M
Melon and Parma ham 8
Meringue nests 33
Mince pies 38
Mousses
  chicken liver mousse 8
  lemon mousse 31
Mushrooms
  ham and mushroom rolls 56
  marinated mushrooms 41
  mushroom filo tartlets 8

N
Napkin garlands 64
Nuts
  fruit and nut caramels 40
  port and nut stuffing 18
  rice and nut stuffing 10

O
Oranges
  apricot and orange relish 15
  citrus broccoli and cauliflower 22
  cranberry and clementine cake 50
  duck with orange sauce 17
  orange and brandy butter 37

P
Parsnips
  puffed parsnip 25

roast parsnips 24
Peach cup 62
Pears, festive poached 32
Pineapple
   fluffy pineapple sauce 28
Pizza, three cheese 58
Pork, serving 69
Potatoes
   ham and potato cakes 57
   railroad potatoes 25
   rosemary potatoes 22
Poussin, serving 69

R
Relish, apricot and orange 15
Rice and nut stuffing 10

S
Salad
   crispy bacon and avocado salad 6
   ham and turkey Niçoise 56
Salmon
   smoked salmon parcels 6
   striped salmon terrine 4
Sauces
   bread sauce 13
   clear brandy sauce 37
   duck with orange sauce 17
   fluffy pineapple sauce 28
   honey apple sauce 13
   spicy cranberry sauce 13
   Cumberland sauce 13
Sausages
   bacon-wrapped 12
   sausage rolls 41
Shortbread jewels 40
Soufflés
   iced Cointreau soufflé 32
   leek and stilton soufflé 4
Soup
   cauliflower and cress soup 8
   chestnut and cranberry soup 7
   Roquefort and almond soup 8
Strawberry cup 62
Stuffing
   apple and hazelnut stuffing 13
   cheese 16
   oaty stuffing balls 12
   port and nut stuffing 18
   rice and nut stuffing 10
   tarragon and parsley 16

T
Table decorations 63-65
Terrine, striped salmon 4
Tomatoes, beans with 24
Trifle, apricot sherry 35
Turkey
   accompaniments 12
   carving 67
   ham and turkey Niçoise 56
   perfect roast turkey 10
   roasting 67
   stock 68
   storing and reheating 67
   stuffing 66
   thawing 66
   trussing 66
   turkey and chutney loaf 58
   turkey creole 59

V
Vegetables
   crudités with garlic dip 6
   vegetarian filo slice 20

W
Watercress
   cauliflower and cress soup 9
   stilton and watercress tart 58
Wiring decorations 64